IMPRESARIO

IMPRESARIO
MALCOLM MCLAREN AND THE BRITISH NEW WAVE

PAUL TAYLOR
Guest Curator

THE NEW MUSEUM OF CONTEMPORARY ART
NEW YORK

•

THE MIT PRESS
CAMBRIDGE, MASSACHUSETTS; LONDON, ENGLAND

Impresario: Malcolm McLaren and the British New Wave, an exhibition at The New Museum of Contemporary Art, New York, September 16–November 20, 1988.

Funding for this exhibition and catalogue has been generously provided by Jay Chiat, and the National Endowment for the Arts, a federal agency. Programs at The New Museum also receive operating support from the New York State Council on the Arts, and the New York City Department of Cultural Affairs as well as from many corporations, foundations and individuals.

The individual views expressed in the exhibition and catalogue are not necessarily those of the Museum.

TABLE OF CONTENTS

6 PREFACE AND ACKNOWLEDGMENTS
Marcia Tucker and William Olander

11 THE IMPRESARIO OF DO-IT-YOURSELF
Paul Taylor

31 FROM *LET IT ROCK* TO *WORLD'S END*: 430 KING'S ROAD
Jane Withers

45 THE GREAT ROCK 'N' ROLL SWINDLE
Jon Savage

59 MALCOLM MCLAREN AND THE MAKING OF ANNABELLA
Dan Graham

72 CHRONOLOGY
Compiled by Malcolm McLaren

74 LIST OF ILLUSTRATIONS

CONTRIBUTORS

Editor
Paul Taylor

Assistant Editor
Karen Fiss

Exhibition Design
Judith Barry and Ken Saylor

Catalogue Design
Anthony McCall Associates, New York

Paul Taylor is the founding editor and publisher of *Art & Text* Magazine.

Jane Withers is a London-based writer on design.

Jon Savage is the author of the forthcoming book about the Sex Pistols entitled, *England's Dreaming*.

Dan Graham is an artist and writer living in New York.

LENDERS TO THE EXHIBITION

Adam Ant

Joseph Corre

The Costume Institute, The Metropolitan Museum of Art, New York

Spider Fawke

Lyn Healy

Andrea Linz

Greil Marcus

Malcolm McLaren

Ted Muehling

The Noose, New York

Marco Pirroni

Jon Savage

Helen Wellington-Lloyd

Virgin Records Limited

Simon Withers

PREFACE AND ACKNOWLEDGMENTS

In April 1985, Paul Taylor wrote to us with the following proposal: "a retrospective exhibition of the work of Malcolm McLaren. My ideas for the exhibition are quite unconventional, as is McLaren's 'art'." Though we were familiar with McLaren's brilliant pastiche, the album *Fans* released in 1984, and with his role as the manager of the Sex Pistols, his activities as a fashion designer, with Vivienne Westwood, graphic designer, with Jamie Reid and Nick Egan, and as a screenwriter, songwriter, and cultural theorist were not nearly so well known. Add to our unfamiliarity with McLaren's full career the fact that what was being proposed was not an "art exhibition" in any conventional sense, it was clear that we were faced with a most challenging proposal: an exhibition of pop artifacts (clothes, record covers, posters, music and video tapes, films, etc.) associated with an individual who, to many, is not an artist at all but a master manipulator, the "Svengali of punk."

Had Paul Taylor suggested an exhibition of, say, rock musician David Byrne, or performance artist Laurie Anderson, both celebrated figures of the "downtown scene," we probably could have reached a decision rather quickly. Yet, after talking with our colleagues, a decision was reached after little discussion—we wanted to do this exhibition. That it took three years to implement the project is evidence only of the unconventional nature of the show and the logistical problems faced by an institution accustomed to dealing with the most "radical" art but not entirely comfortable with a T-shirt on which two naked cowboys are depicted.

Although The New Museum has occasionally touched on issues of popular culture and commodity culture (for instance, in the recent exhibitions, *Damaged Goods* and *Fake*), never in its eleven-year history has it devoted an entire show to the contents of popular culture or to an artist (and collaborators) whose achievements reside firmly in the arena of mass culture rather than High Culture. From this point of view, *Impresario: Malcolm McLaren and the British New Wave* is a departure. But from the point of view of postmodernist theory and practice, issues on which The New Museum has frequently focused, the exhibition makes perfect sense.

According to certain postmodernist theories, the traditional modernist avant-garde no longer exists, having exhausted itself or, in its turn, having been co-opted by the forms of popular culture. Some have even called this process a democratization of culture whereby popular forms replace those of the bourgeois avant-garde. Or perhaps it is more a matter of displacement—that slippery moment when art becomes commerce, shifting back again into the cultural arena as another kind of commodity. The catch is, even today, in 1988, few among us are willing to acknowledge that certain mass cultural forms and practices may comprise the most significant "culture" of our time, precisely because of their "popular" character. Although many in the community of art may be distressed by our view of Malcolm McLaren as an "artist," we believe that *Impresario: Malcolm McLaren and the British New Wave*, like many other New Museum projects, will challenge and ultimately expand our accepted notions of what constitutes art.

Our thanks first to Malcolm McLaren, for his patience and many contributions to this most complicated project; Paul Taylor, for creating the exhibition and his skillful manipulation of its details; Jon Savage, for his assistance in London; the lenders, who are listed elsewhere in this catalogue, for agreeing to part with cherished artifacts; the contributors to this catalogue, whose essays add an enormously significant component to the exhibition; and to Norman Rosenthal and the Royal Academy of Arts, for their attempts to present *Impresario: Malcolm McLaren and the British New Wave* in London. We also would like to thank Anthony McCall and his associates for the exciting design of the catalogue, and Judith Barry and Ken Saylor for their innovative design of the exhibition itself. We are pleased that MIT Press has agreed to distribute this catalogue, and thank Roger Conover for his efforts on our behalf. Finally, special thanks to A/T Scharff Rentals for assistance with the audio portion of the exhibition, and Greneker and Company for their generous donation of mannequins.

At The New Museum, many staff members provided their skill and expertise. Karen Fiss, Curatorial Coordinator, was responsible for many of the details of the exhibition, and was instrumental in the realization of this catalogue. Alice Yang skillfully saw the project through to completion. Providing essential assistance were Teresa Bramlette, Curatorial Secretary, Jeanne Breitbart, Lydia Yee, Mimi Young, and Marina Rustow. Jill Newmark, Registrar, and Cindy Smith, Chief Preparator, were invaluable in coordinating the loans, shipping, and complex installation. Virginia Strull, Director of Planning and Development, diligently pursued funding for the exhibition. Susan Cahan, Russell Ferguson and Sara Palmer organized the public programs in conjunction with the show, and Gayle Kurtz graciously pursued in-kind sponsorship. In addition, the staff members in each department all made significant contributions towards the success of this special project.

We are especially grateful to Jay Chiat, and to the National Endowment for the Arts, a federal agency, for their generous support of this exhibition. Laura Skoler and Jay Chiat have provided hospitality and welcome to the artist and others, and sponsored some of the opening festivities.

The following individuals and organizations also have contributed in a number of special ways: Robyn Beeche, Big Apple Lights Corp., David Bishop, Carol Ann Blinken, Brooklyn Academy of Music, Sonya Cardy, Simon Draper and Virgin Records Limited, Diana Edkins, Nick Egan, Richard Ekstract, Bob Gruen, Michael Halsband, Mark Kloth, Richard Knox, Annie Leibovitz, Virginia Lohle, Richard Martin, Harold Koda and the Fashion Institute of Technology, Luciana Martinez de la Rosa, Eugene Mosier, Jeff Schock, John Kevin Sutton, Julien Temple, Patricia Thornley, Variety Scenic Studios and many others.

Marcia Tucker
Director

William Olander
Senior Curator

THE IMPRESARIO OF DO-IT-YOURSELF
Paul Taylor

*My name is Malcolm McLaren. I have brought you many things in my time... but the most successful of all was an invention of mine they called punk rock.*

Malcolm McLaren didn't invent punk. All he did was envisage it, design it, clothe it, publicize it and sell it. In the film *The Great Rock 'n' Roll Swindle*, he appears in a black rubber garment and mask of his own design and whispers the above in a conspiratorial voice. There begins the story of how he swindled a fortune from the British music industry.

The Great Rock 'n' Roll Swindle is a *grand guignol* performance about the rise and fall of the Sex Pistols. A primer of corporate subversion, its poisonous message is dressed up as a musical about the infamous punk band that McLaren managed from 1975 to 1979. But like the ten little indians, the Sex Pistols split away one by one during the making of the movie, and McLaren was all that was left. Then, when the film was almost in the can, he ran away too. Punk was finished.

In those days, Malcolm McLaren's motto was "Cash from Chaos." He was a peddler of people and ideas, an incendiary ideas-man who created a tidal wave of bad feelings, misspent cash and stunned publicity. He certainly helped to politicize rock and roll. Yet like the solitary traveler, the dandy and the picaresque *raconteur* of romantic times, there is something about McLaren that is compellingly artistic.

Former art student, fashion designer, band manager, songwriter, singer, record and film producer, tastemaker and irrepressible litigant, his activism in the Pop music world demands a reckoning within the artistic development of our century. McLaren's 'art' (that is, his way of combining the arts) is comparable to the contributions of F.T. Marinetti, Serge Diaghilev and Andy Warhol. Within the world of Pop, McLaren is dubbed a vampiric Svengali, con-man and fake artist. *The Times* of London labeled McLaren the "Proud Pirate of Punk" and Matthew Ashman (a member of the formerly McLaren-managed group, Bow Wow Wow) branded him the "Shylock of Rock." Boy George, who was engaged by McLaren to sing with Bow Wow Wow while still an unknown, says, "he's very clever, but he takes the credit for everything, including the things he never touched."[1]

Clearly, Malcolm McLaren is a "bad guy" of contemporary pop culture, a reputation that in these times makes him all the more appealing. To many in the worlds of art and social criticism, however, McLaren is like a new type of artist. A "producer" in more than one sense of the word, he has literally orchestrated new musical events and created provocative "cultural texts" within the mass-media. He has also shown that art in the post-avant-garde era is a matter of synthesis, of combining elements from radically different sources. Inspired by the artistic avant-gardes of the 1910s, McLaren has applied the artistic methods and ideologies of the Cubists, Futurists, Dadaists and Constructivists to everyday life and spectacular popular culture alike. McLaren is a popularizer, which is to say that he is a pioneer.

"I learned all my politics and understanding of the world through the history of art," McLaren said in a television documentary about his career.[2] He has also explained that while he was a student, "art schools were islands of the dispossessed. I discovered an incredible critique that has stayed with me up to today." In fact, McLaren's discovery of this "incredible critique," no matter how naively or incompletely he grasped it, has created a continuity between the radical avant-garde artists and the pop world of today—from the Futurists, Dadaists, Surrealists and Situationists through to the media subversives of the 1960s and beyond.

1. THE SOLO ARTIST

. . . if I'm starved for blood I look like a perfect horror—skin shrunken, veins like ropes over the contours of my bones.

But I don't let that happen now. And the only consistent indication that I'm not human is my fingernails. It's the same with all vampires . . .

Right now I am what America calls a Rock Superstar. My first album has sold 4 million copies. I'm going to San Francisco for the first spot on a nationwide concert tour that will take my band from coast to coast. MTV, the rock music cable channel, has been playing my video clips night and day for two weeks. They're also being shown in England on "Top of the Pops" and on the continent, probably in some parts of Asia, and in Japan. Video cassettes of the whole series of clips are selling worldwide.

Finally I came to my decision . . .

It is not enough any longer that my little rock band be successful. . . . We must create a fame that will carry my name and my voice to the remotest parts of the world.

Anne Rice, *The Vampire Lestat*, 1985

●

In 1983, already famous as the former manager of the Sex Pistols and Bow Wow Wow, McLaren took an unprecedented step—unprecedented among managers of rock bands and entrepreneurs in general—of transforming himself into his own product. More than one reporter remarked that McLaren, "couldn't sing, he couldn't dance, he wasn't young and he wasn't good looking."³ Yet, with £100,000 and the record producer Trevor Horn, McLaren traveled to Africa, New York and the American South, picking up ideas and soundtracks for a new album. The resulting record mixed all the sounds together. In the manner of a radio listener who is incessantly switching the dial, McLaren's first solo effort, *Duck Rock*, created a new kind of musical collage. By returning to the source of rock and roll music—the African beat—McLaren took it a step further. *Duck Rock* caught the pop world by surprise and shot the former behind-the-scenes agitator to personal stardom.

Duck Rock's gimmick was the new trend that had already surfaced in New York: dubbing. Formerly the domain of discjockeys who mixed strains from different records together and therefore made a 'live' performance out of pre-existing records, McLaren's record advocated the use of this technique for everybody. Calling it by its other name, 'scratching' (possibly in reference to the experimental scratch films of the 1960s), McLaren made dubbing both the method and the content of his music.

"Buffalo Gals," the first single from the album, was issued with these instructions on the record cover:

Two manual decks and a rhythm box are all you need. Get a bunch of good rhythm records, choose your favorite parts and groove along with the rhythm machine. Use your hands, scratch the record by repeating the grooves you dig so much. Fade one record into another and keep that rhythm box going. Now start talking and singing over the record with the microphone. Now you're making your own music out of other people's records. That's what scratching is.

In other words, dubbing was promoted by McLaren as a new form of DIY (Do-It-Yourself).

Duck Rock, which synthesized rap, Zulu, Latin and Burundi rhythms, Appalachian hillbilly music and the radio patter of a pair of discjockeys called the World's Famous Supreme Team, was made possible by advances in recording technology. The opportunities created by multi-tracking, synthesized drum machines, emulators and digital samplers mean that records no longer need to be slavish re-presentations of live or studio performances. Instead, as McLaren proposed, the record itself can be used as a musical instrument. "It's using the debris of old music," he explained. "Finding little beats inside other people's records and mixing them together ... doesn't follow the old-fashioned format of verse-chorus ... it goes off at tangents. That's what makes it one of the most inventive, the newest

MCLAREN IN TENNESSEE, 1983.

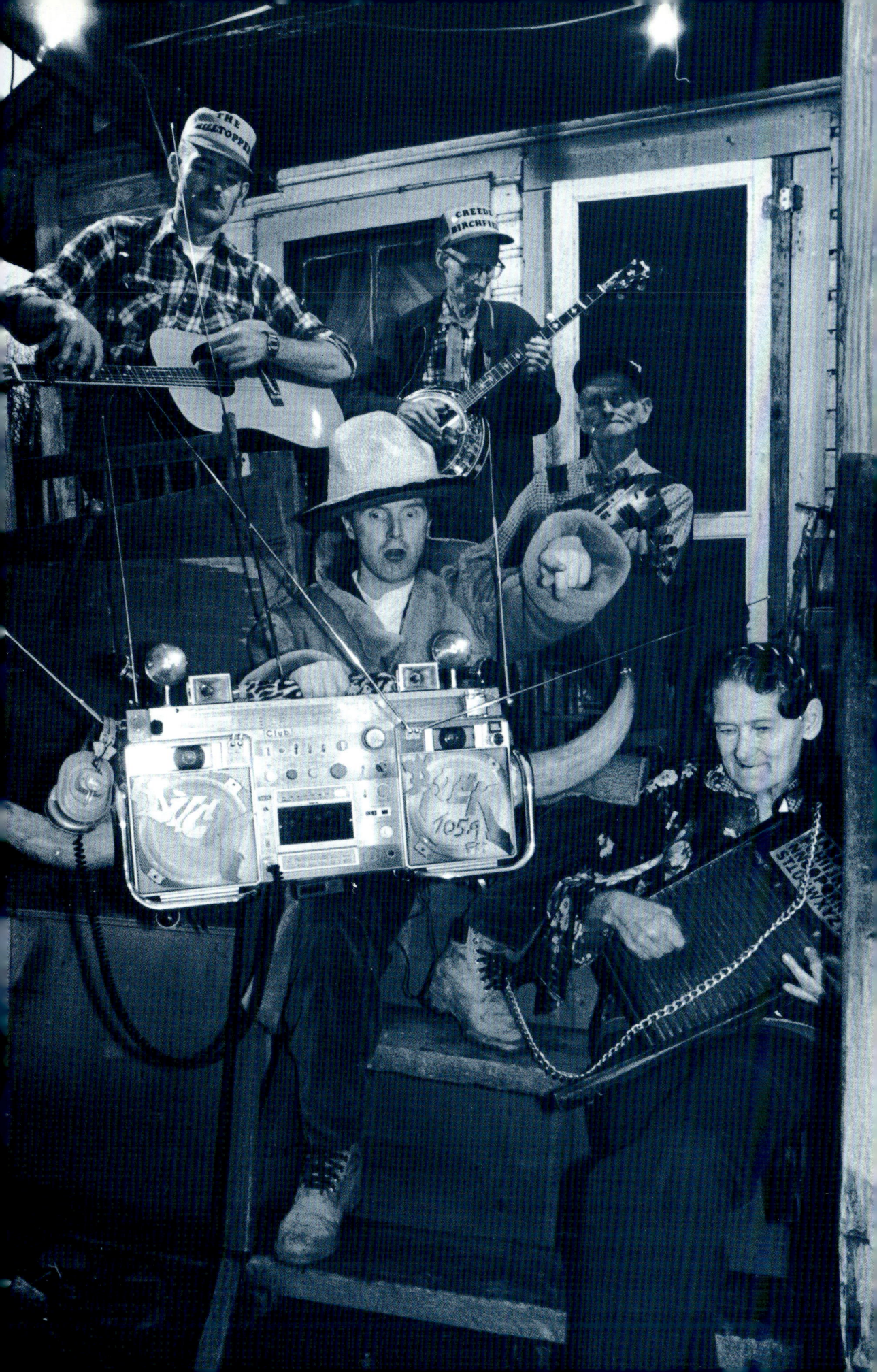

and the most interesting types of music being made today. Scratching is probably the newest urban folk music."⁴

McLaren adorned his first solo album with graphics by Keith Haring, jumping wholeheartedly onto the marketing bandwagon that was pushing the newly trendy manifestations of New York street culture—rap music, breakdancing and graffiti art. When his next record, *Fans,* was released in 1984, melodies from Puccini and Bizet operas were similarly reworked with a dance beat, and McLaren's reputation as an artistic appropriator, a media scavenger, was cemented. (His forthcoming waltz album continues this idea: the proto-disco "Philadelphia Sound" of Barry White's Love Unlimited Orchestra is re-mixed with original material, a tamed House sound and refrains from Johann Strauss and Rodgers and Hammerstein's *The King and I.*)

All the albums, especially *Duck Rock,* have drawn complaints about McLaren's practice of appropriation. (In fact, he was sued by the white South African owners of the copyright of the black music used on *Duck Rock,* although he had paid the musicians themselves.) McLaren told his critics:

*All I can say is that accusations of plagiarism don't bother me. As far as I'm concerned it's all I'm useful for, but if people don't want me to plagiarize I'll have to stop work... I can't sit down and write a tune. I'm not interested. I can't write a tune as good [sic] as Puccini, so why bother? I can't write a soulful rendition with a big African rhythm like the Zulu, so why bother? Why not go and join them and bring it back because people here are so blinkered?*⁵

Apart from their entertainment value, McLaren's albums are valuable for the way they recast the role of the producer in music. For him, production takes precedence over performance. This emphasizes (after Duchamp's readymades) that composition is a process of selection and synthesis—of creative listening, and not necessarily a mystifying artistic process of coming-into-being. In typical pop and rock and roll music, by contrast, the performer is the focus of the work as well as the locus of its meaning (similar to the role of the painter in expressionist and action painting). McLaren's music makes its own piecemeal construction intelligible, less opaque and more participatory. The affective role of both the producer and the consumer had become McLaren's *idée fixe.*

2. THE POP ARTIST

Malcolm McLaren's popular art adds up to something that was supposed to have passed with the sixties. With his collaborators since the mid-1970s, including his former *de facto* wife and fellow clothes designer Vivienne Westwood, the bands the Sex Pistols and Bow Wow Wow and others, he is one of the missing links between avant-garde and contemporary art. If we can restore this link, contemporary art's present sense of absolute gratuitousness may be mitigated.

Moreover, the cynical marketing of artists and works of art since the 1960s has forced increasing numbers of artists and critics to look at the mechanisms of presentation within the culture industry and assess the role of the merchandiser. As the producer's role is recognized as being of increasingly greater importance, McLaren's position becomes pivotal.

The New Wave subculture of the 1970s, in the words of one ex-punk journalist, "had a social conscience that was embarrassingly like that of the Hippies." It was ultimately "all radical style and no content." Yet it was also "a marvelous career opportunity for a sizable number of disaffected youth on the fringes of show-business."[6] Seizing this opportunity, punk and New Wave designers contributed enormously to their different media. Most pervasive on the level of materials and appearances were certain of punk's DIY methods: cutting-up and re-using pre-existing materials. Such "bricolage" was applied to clothes, jewelry, graphics, and music.[7] It was an artistic breakthrough that arrived with amazing aplomb. Originally cheap, punk has become an expensive fashion ticket. Yet its position at the cutting edge of style has not abated; punk design and iconography feature prominently in the 1988 collections of designers such as Jean-Paul Gaultier in Paris and Stephen Sprouse in New York. Like the contribution of Pop Art, punk's influence is evident in the other arts as well.

The spirit as well as the imagery of punk is behind most of the contemporary developments in the 1980s art world. Punk provided the neo-expressionist art movement with its destructive, apocalyptic attitude and self-consciously bad manners, and predated its violently broken surfaces and juxtapositions of incongruous styles. Graffiti art, which surfaced in the New York art scene in the late 1970s, was equipped with a sense of guerrilla tactics and outrageous social mobility that punk had pre-ordained. Jamie Reid's photomontages and graphics for record covers look remarkably similar to recent work by numerous New York photo-and-text artists. And today's neo-pop has definitely taken from the lyrics of many punk bands (and their manner of packaging themselves) its cunning about the business of culture and conviction about contemporary art's inescapable commodification. Punk binds Pop Art to the postmodernism of the 1980s.

3. THE YOUNG ARTIST

Malcolm McLaren studied art over an eight-year period during the 1960s. He attended three art colleges and, briefly, Chiswick Polytechnic (which is associated with the London Academy of Music and Dramatic Art), and recalls that his teachers included Peter Blake, William Tucker, Frank Auerbach, Andrew Forge and Peter Cresswell. McLaren was an extremely distracted student; Jamie Reid, who later became the graphic designer for the Sex Pistols, met him in 1968 around the time that the board of governors at Croydon College tried to have McLaren committed to an asylum for the insane.[8]

A libertarian activist, McLaren landed at Goldsmiths' College in 1969 and, as Peter Cresswell, who is now Dean of Goldsmiths' art school remembers:

He arrived from under a cloud of some sort. His name was Malcolm Edwards in those days, and he wasn't particularly stylish—he just dressed like an art student. The one thing you can say about McLaren was that he was extremely aggressive, unusually aggressive. It was not physical aggression, it was just his style. Malcolm developed a trick early on of not behaving the way you think he would—it was ever so slightly disturbing. And he would stimulate a confrontation, just to see how people behaved.[9]

Goldsmiths' College was also the art school which McLaren and others disrupted in 1970 with a free-cultural weekend festival of music, performance art, films and seminars on political and psychoanalytic themes. McLaren was fervently inspired by the May '68 student riots in Paris and the Hornsey/London School of Economics sit-ins. Since then, his politics are as if frozen in time. While they are still decadent and libertarian, they are also pre-feminist.

According to Cresswell, Pop Art was "dying" at the end of the 1960s, at which time McLaren made monochromatic shaped canvases that approached "environmental" proportions. His first exhibition was held at the now-defunct Kingly Street Gallery. It was a maze of cardboard in which gallery visitors, who entered it in the expectation of seeing art, would become lost.

In 1968 he started to make a 16mm film on the history of Oxford Street in London, the thoroughfare that had been redesigned after the Gordon Riots of the 1780s so as to inhibit crowds from gaining access to important parts of the city. McLaren was interested in filming this semi-documentary, "from a crowd-gathering and social, political

INSTALLATION, MALCOLM MCLAREN, 1967.

MCLAREN AT CROYDON COLLEGE OF ART, 1968.

point of view," he says, "to watch how crowds and people are manipulated, and the whole consumer aspect of society."

McLaren's years at art school were also memorable for his demand that the students be given gold to carve.[10] At most they received a government grant, and McLaren says:

I spent most of my grant buying records. When I realized that I had accumulated over 3,000 rock and roll records, I decided to hump them off down King's Road in a shop.... I also thought that I should start to sell clothes, and not having the money, I decided to thieve all of the equipment out of my old art college—all the film equipment. I managed to do a deal with an old friend of mine who was running the student union at a competitive art institute and he bought it all with students' funds, giving me an incredible price. From there on in I was in business.

It was great fun, because I suddenly didn't have to consider the idea of painting. I just had to consider the idea of selling. And selling things became an art in itself. The idea was provocation.... I got very artistic and suddenly started tearing holes in T-shirts and borrowing phrases from Alex Trocchi's porno novels.... Lo and behold, we (Vivienne Westwood and I) changed the shop from being somewhat of a "retro" shop into another shop called Sex. *It was about demystifying that whole experience that was absolutely frowned upon and only sold in brown bags—that is, rubber and leather clothing. Suddenly the whole shop was a huge fetish parade and I had these kids walking out with rubber skirts on and leather jeans and dog collars, and holding whips and chains and wearing little tit clamps over their nipples. Some got arrested and some didn't. I realized then that I was on the cutting edge of fashion.*

4. THE MANAGER

... a very old shrivelled Jew, whose villanous looking and repulsive face was obscured by a quantity of matted red hair. [Fagan] was dressed in a greasy flannel gown, with his throat bare, and seemed to be dividing his time between the frying-pan and the clothes-horse, over which a great number of silk handkerchiefs were hanging. Several rough beds made of old sacks were huddled side by side on the floor. Seated around the table were four or five boys.

Charles Dickens, *Oliver Twist*, 1837-9

●

The New York Dolls were McLaren's first opportunity to realize a fantasy that was inspired by his flirtation with Situationist politics in London at the close of the 1960s. Situationism, a Surrealist-inspired political movement in France that was formed in the mid-1950s from the International Lettrists, the Society for an Imaginist Bauhaus and the COBRA movement (comprising artists from Copenhagen, Brussels and Amsterdam), was largely responsible for the rhetoric and imagery of the May '68 revolts in Paris.

In London, McLaren had become interested in a group called King Mob, named after a famous bit of graffiti that had appeared on the Newgate prison during the Gordon Riots. King Mob published *Echo*, a small magazine that included translations from the Situationist Guy Debord and various writings about psychiatry, crime and sedition in general. Many of the magazine's graphics, and some of its covers, employed imagery that was to re-appear in McLaren's boutiques—leather guerrilla gear, altered cartoons and slogans (which he printed onto T-shirts and handkerchiefs).

Associated with King Mob were, among others, Christopher Gray, the Wise brothers, young art historian T.J. Clark and Jamie Reid. While Clark, for example, now refers to McLaren as "boring-old-McNasty," Reid became his graphic artist.[11] Reid, who was working as a lay-out artist for the left-wing Suburban Press, received a telegram from McLaren in March 1976, requesting his services for the Sex Pistols.

Already, Christopher Gray had floated the idea of a "totally unpleasant" anti-music pop band; some ancient graffiti near Victoria Coach station still reads, "Chris Gray Band." This, of course, was the era of experimentalism in the arts, and conceptual links between art and pop music were already in place. In the galleries, artistic protest about art was more or less the status quo. It was decades earlier that Andre Breton, the impresario of Surrealism, had declared that, "in the bad taste of my time I wish to go further than anybody." In 1965, Andy Warhol's film, *Vinyl*, based on Anthony Burgess' novel, *A Clockwork Orange*, depicted a small band of punks. (As filmed by Stanley Kubrick in 1971, the story heralded the onset of punk in Britain. Indeed, Britain's punks were to assume the practice that Warhol had pinched from the Hollywood studios, dubbing themselves with patently artificial new names.) By 1974, when McLaren went to New York and took on the management of the New York Dolls, the taste for anti-artistic manifestations and "subversions" was widespread and financially lucrative.

McLaren said that on first hearing a tape of the band, "I thought it was the worst record I'd ever heard ... [But] it didn't matter that the music was so bad. What mattered was that they were so good at being bad.... That gave me a whole other attitude towards music that I didn't have. It locked in my own thoughts about what was important

STILL FROM WARHOL'S *VINYL*, 1965.

FIRST ISSUE COVER, APRIL 1968.

... the presentation of it all, the attitude and the fact that you didn't have to be good."[12] Evidently, the Dolls' fans agreed with him, because in 1973, readers of both *Creem* and *Circus* magazines had voted the Dolls the best new band of 1973, while readers of *Creem* also voted them the worst.

The extent of McLaren's influence on the New York Dolls varies from account to account. McLaren was manager for the band's last six months. But his contribution was not restricted to booking their engagements. He created for them a pseudo-political image by redesigning their already outrageous costumes, fitting them in red patent leather outfits. Moreover, he couched this new "Maoist" look in art rhetoric: "What are the politics of boredom?" asked McLaren's first press release. He called it a Manifesto.

On his return to London in 1975, McLaren formed the Sex Pistols. Initially, the new group was supposed to publicize *Sex*, the newest incarnation of the store that McLaren shared with Vivienne Westwood. "There had to be a music that went with the clothes," he said. "The Sex Pistols provided the sound—anarchic, shrill, garage-like. It wasn't important that they could play. It was more important the way they dressed and how they looked."[13]

Johnny Rotten met McLaren and Westwood at *Sex* and became the lead singer of the group. He also penned many of the band's lyrics. The other members—Steve Jones and Paul Cook, and Glen Matlock who was replaced in 1977 by Sid Vicious—had also been gleaned from the same fashionably outcast store on the World's End strip of King's Road. The 29-year-old manager had no idea of what the Sex Pistols would become, but as soon as he realized they were not the new Rolling Stones, he set about to make them a wicked, hateable, thoroughly "bad" version of CBS's invention, the Monkees.

From their initial appearance at St. Martin's School of Art at the end of 1975 to January 1978, when Johnny Rotten left the band, and then on to February 1979, when Sid Vicious died of an overdose, the Sex Pistols story turned out to be more spectacular than McLaren had ever envisioned. The band scandalized Britain, enjoyed a three-year reign of media terror and quickly became an historic moment in Pop music.

The Sex Pistols' first appearance on television, in December 1976, featured a few expletives whose utterance shot the four young men to national infamy. TV interviewer Bill Grundy had made a suggestion to one of the women accompanying the band that, "We'll meet afterwards, shall we?" to which Johnny Rotten replied, "You dirty sod.

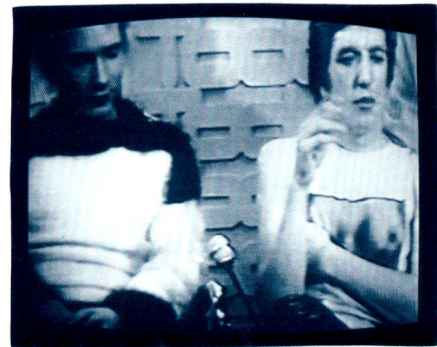

JOHNNY ROTTEN & STEVE JONES ON BOB GRUNDY'S "TODAY" SHOW, LONDON, 1976.

SINGLE COVER, DESIGN BY JAMIE REID, 1977.

You dirty old man." Grundy retorted, "Well, keep going chief, keep going. (Pause) Go on. You've got another five seconds. Say something outrageous."
"You dirty bastard."
"Go on, again."
"You dirty fucker."
"What a clever boy."
"What a fucking rotter."

This simple "speech act" earned the band, and McLaren, the role of spokespersons for Britain's disaffected, unemployed and stylish youth. The television station was inundated with complaints, and the tabloids had found a new subject that was sordid enough for their readership. The punk scandal was underway. Virtually banned from performing live and on the air, and shielded from the press by their manager, the Sex Pistols became the object of official curiosity. Enigma and outrage became the band's selling points.

5. THE CON-ARTIST

Less than two months earlier, in October, McLaren had signed the Sex Pistols to EMI records for £40,000. McLaren saw this initial commercial breakthrough as the foundation stone of his corporate swindle, as well as an amazing affront to the artistic standards of the rock industry which was still in the grip of arty album-oriented rock. And mindful of Dickens' Scrooge, whom he numbers among his heroes, McLaren reluctantly increased the payment to the individual band-members from £25 to £35 per week. He explained, "'Well, what do you need money for? You'll only be stupid, you'll only spend it. You're having a grand old time.' I always put them in good hotels though. I was always good about that."[14] But due to such shocking, headline-grabbing behavior as on the Grundy show, the band—and McLaren's company, Glitterbest Ltd.—were released from their contract with EMI. (The corporation itself soon became the subject of one of the Sex Pistols' lyrics.)

Two months after this initial rift, during the preparations for Queen Elizabeth II's Jubilee, A & M Records signed the band for the release of "God Save The Queen," a typically ironic New Wave insult, for £75,000. But after one week, the band's carefully orchestrated and choreographed misbehavior proved too controversial for the image of this company as well, and the new contract was severed. In defense of its actions, A & M representatives cited numerous complaints against the band, many of which in fact had been made anonymously from McLaren's office.

Next, the by-now notorious manager signed the group to a relatively small, new company, Virgin Records, for £45,000 and to Barclay records in France for £26,000. For world publishing rights (except North America), Warner Brothers paid £100,000. Arista paid

ANIMATION FROM *THE GREAT ROCK 'N' ROLL SWINDLE*, 1979–80.

£100,000 for North America. Then McLaren accepted an additional £200,000 from Warner Brothers towards an album, which he says he accepted only because the corporation made a commitment to his proposed Sex Pistols movie. Virgin paid another £75,000 towards the movie and, eventually, says McLaren, another £100,000 after he threatened to take the band elsewhere. But it is possible that, due to subsequent events, McLaren's company never actually handled Virgin's last installment.

At each new signing, McLaren tipped off the press to the irony that, although they were banned from the radio and public performances, and while they had barely cut a record, the Sex Pistols were reaping enormous profits. He quipped, "the Sex Pistols are like some crazy disease—untouchable. I keep walking in and out of offices being given checks. When I'm older and people ask me what I used to do for a living I shall have to say, 'I went in and out of doors getting paid for it.'" At the end of 1977, it was no surprise to see the Sex Pistols dubbed "Young Businessmen of the Year" and their photograph gracing the cover of the British weekly, *Investor's Review*.

As a commercial venture, however, punk actually eluded the grip of the music corporations. Eventually even McLaren realized, as he says,

Punk rock couldn't be sold. . . . It was too much to do with Do-It-Yourself. As soon as you get a Do-It-Yourself force out there, you spawn 5,000 other groups. The record industry never wanted 5,000 groups. They only want one group. One group is more manageable. It's one dictator telling you what the culture is all about rather than 5,000. They don't like the socialist idea that everyone can do it.

Of course, in a scene in which "everyone can do it," the producer's role becomes all-important, and ever aware of this, McLaren was slow to consider the interests of the individual bandmembers. He concentrated instead on his media spectacle. So when the lead singer of the Sex Pistols, Johnny Rotten, brought suit against him for the proceeds of the band's exploits, the man only recently dubbed the 'Diaghilev of Punk,' was incensed. This dramatic final chapter of punk, which was initiated in January 1978 and concluded only in 1986, was a court battle between the surviving members of the band and their manager. The dispute assumed the proportions of a philosophical enquiry: Who is the rightful owner of a pop event?

On the eve of the band's break-up, McLaren hatched his final scheme—the Sex Pistols film. But it did not turn out to be The World According to Malcolm

SINGLE COVER, DESIGN BY JAMIE REID, 1977.

"YOUNG BUSINESSMEN OF THE YEAR," 1977.

McLaren that he had intended. He had originally scripted, with Roger Ebert and others, a movie to be directed by Russ Meyer. In it, McLaren would portray himself as "a man in his mid-30s who fancies himself as the nation's leading and most uncanny Trend spotter . . . the ultimate eclectic." His character was to "lurk in the shadows" and utter such rallying cries as, "I'm the tycoon of pop! . . . Downtrodden rock, that's what's next! Music for a nation out of work! Smash the system and get rich doing it, that's my motto."[15]

Instead of this film, entitled *Anarchy In The U.K.* and then a second script, *Who Killed Bambi?*, quite a different film was realized: *The Great Rock 'n' Roll Swindle* directed by Julien Temple. The new film cleverly combines documentary footage of the band with animation and a more or less true story about the Sex Pistols. As Jamie Reid recalled, the film was intended "to be a loud and blatant statement about consumerism and who buys pop records and what a pop band is—just a factory churning out things for people to buy, but surrounded by myth."[16] Then, during the editing of the film, Sid Vicious was arraigned for the killing of his girlfriend Nancy Spungeon and, soon after, died himself of a heroin overdose. (Within the few weeks that separated the two incidents, McLaren issued Sid Vicious T-shirts that read, "I'm Alive. She's Dead. I'm Yours," and reportedly attempted to negotiate book and film rights to the Sid Vicious story.)[17] New animated sequences were added to *The Great Rock 'n' Roll Swindle* to bring the saga up to date.

Johnny Rotten refused to participate in the film, and as Julien Temple and McLaren (as co-producer) were completing it, he instigated legal proceedings against his former manager. Without informing even Westwood, McLaren quickly fled to Paris (although he was not in such a hurry, he says, to forget to pass by his bank and withdraw as much cash as possible from the Sex Pistols accounts).

Although *The Great Rock 'n' Roll Swindle* achieved minor cult status in Britain and other countries (it has never been released in the United States), it was a bitter disappointment to McLaren. To be sure, it presents him as the brains behind the band and tells his version of the 'Swindle' in ten lessons—"How To Manufacture Your Group," "How To Steal As Much Money As Possible From The Record Company Of Your Choice," "Cultivate Hatred; It's Your Biggest Asset," etc. To McLaren however, the film was a sadly-missed opportunity, a shoddy compromise.

While in "exile," he wrote a private correspondence to the film's producers:

FROM *THE GREAT ROCK 'N' ROLL SWINDLE*, 1979–80.

I believe that the film is in no better shape than a completely misdirected rough cut which makes no sense at all. [It] does not work for a number of reasons, but the major and extremely serious one is the film's total disregard in providing the one possible anchor for the audience; that is, two people telling the same story from different points of view. These two people are Steve Jones, a lone typical cliche crook, and McLaren, an underground fetish Lucifer, both part of the Sex Pistols.

His letter was five pages long and concluded with the demand: "I wish my name to be struck off this film's credits entirely and myself taken out immediately of all scenes.... Your most obedient servant," etc.[18] He wasn't, and there ended the swindle, almost.

6. THE COMMERCIAL ARTIST

The baroque artistic creation's long-lost unity is in some way rediscovered in the current consumption of the totality of past art. When all art is recognized and sought ... the very production of baroque art merges with all its rivals.... Once this 'collection of souvenirs' of art history becomes possible, it is also the end of the work of art.

Guy Debord, *Society of the Spectacle*, 1967

•

Malcolm McLaren's career underwent a significant change after the demise of the Sex Pistols in 1979. While his activities as the manager of the band had been mostly agitational in nature, often without a formal scheme, his work from 1980 to today is set firmly within the perimeters of the fashion and culture industry. Hired for four weeks by Adam Ant, lead singer of the new "post-punk" band Adam and the Ants, McLaren's first task was to revamp the band's image, which he did in tandem with Vivienne Westwood. He made suggestions about the band's outfits as well as its music, combining "Geronimo" Indian face make-up with pirate costumes.

From these same design elements, Westwood and McLaren then launched a new fashion line. Aided by Adam Ant's commercial success, the clothes reached a wider fashion audience than anything they had done before, and Westwood herself set out to enter the international fashion scene. She made a skillful transition from a Do-It-Yourself punk seamstress to a high fashion designer. Gone were the urban primitive's outfits and, in their place, ensued a reign of luxurious musical and artistic quotation, which McLaren calls "gilded punk."

When McLaren's month-long contract with Adam Ant expired, three of the "Ants" defected and formed their own band, which McLaren elected to manage. He then "discovered" Annabella, a teenage lead-singer who reminded him of an extra from *South Pacific*,

ADAM AND THE ANTS ALBUM, 1980.

named the band Bow Wow Wow after the image of the dog on the HMV logo, and signed the package to EMI. (In Britain, HMV is owned by EMI; in the United States, the dog and gramophone logo is owned by RCA, to whom McLaren signed the band when, again, his product was dumped by EMI.) Bow Wow Wow's lyrics, the cleverest of which were penned by McLaren, as well as the presentation of their products and publicity, were calculated affronts to the recording industry in a totally new guise. Among the targets of McLaren's songs were, for example, ownership of musical properties (the single "C30 C60 C90 GO!" advocated home-taping as opposed to buying music) and the work ethic (as in "W.O.R.K. No My Daddy Don't").

While it has been said that Punk Rock "ushered popular music into postmodernism," McLaren's work with Bow Wow Wow was an even more self-conscious artistic gesture.[19] Its parallels to the postmodernism of the early 1980s art world are obvious; McLaren's packaging of Bow Wow Wow, the primitivistic, low-skill sound of their music, their lyrics and McLaren's continuing role as producer evoke the theories of Roland Barthes about the demise of the conventional music text in the grip of new technology. Bow Wow Wow also coincided with the world-wide trend toward textual appropriation, which McLaren called piracy.

From 1980 to 1982, the band was a watershed for McLaren and others (it was as part of Bow Wow Wow that Boy George made his debut). With his new act, McLaren won a degree of recognition as an artist of sorts, and it was from there (following his frustrations with Annabella's inability to behave as imaginatively and rebelliously as Johnny Rotten had) that he resolved to pursue a solo recording career. A year later, he recorded *Duck Rock*.

7. PYGMALION

Two months after Rotten brought suit, the funds which were held by McLaren's companies, Glitterbest and Matrixbest, were placed in the care of the Official Receiver until such time that the dispute was resolved. The amount in question was estimated at 1 million pounds. (In fact, when the royalties from *The Great Rock 'n' Roll Swindle* were added, the amount was almost 1.5 million pounds.) Johnny Rotten resumed the use of his real name, John Lydon. A highly principled, often moralistic, working-class, lapsed Irish Catholic, Lydon is, to say the least, a contrasting figure to McLaren, who is happy to describe himself as a "miserly," irreligious Jew of ancient Portuguese descent. In artistic terms, the pair represents that most contemporary and, in this case, most volatile artistic opposition: that of performer and producer.

JOHNNY ROTTEN, 1978.

The difference between Lydon and McLaren, between the hardworking, holy underdog and his high-brow aesthete-master, was cast by the media as a war of archetypes. Rotten was Oliver Twist to McLaren's Fagan; Lydon was the young blood, McLaren the bloodsucker. Rotten once cried "McLaren is the most evil man alive." But, according to McLaren, "Johnny was a good boy, trying hard to be a bad boy."[20] McLaren also explains that Lydon, "didn't like his name Johnny Rotten. He didn't like his role, but that's what he was employed to be. That was his job.... Rotten has made the whole business of the Sex Pistols seedy and sleazy, and turned the whole thing into an issue of money."

As McLaren tells the story, "In 1979, Rotten, backed by Richard Branson, the Managing Director of Virgin, brought an action in court." Lydon, he says, refused a settlement of £50,000 and insisted on bringing suit.

*The prosecution painted a very black portrait of me. But the judge, after viewing an early version of the film (*The Great Rock 'n' Roll Swindle*) couldn't tell if the whole thing was a joke on him. He didn't know if he was being sent up. You see, originally it was very well written. He asked the prosecution to come to terms with me. He thought that Rotten was trying to be a Jesus Christ. But Rotten wouldn't negotiate, so the judge appointed an independent accountant to oversee the completion of the film—editing out what Rotten and "Mrs. Vicious" [Sid's mother] didn't like, the animated scene of Sid fucking his mother—with Branson cast as her boyfriend.*

"During this period," McLaren claims, "my office was raided by the police. Basement tapes were stolen and sold to Branson, who later released them all on record." By the time the case came back to the courts, the Official Receiver had held the funds for a total of seven years, during which McLaren's and Lydon's careers had drastically altered. Lydon's new band, Public Image Ltd., had made a dramatic appearance, and McLaren's new reputation as a recording artist had also peaked. Also during that period, both men had separately relocated to the last refuge for English scoundrels, Los Angeles.

Alluding to the myth of Pygmalion—he is nothing if not an iconographer—McLaren defends his action. He says he behaved just as an artist should, and "rather than while away my time painting, I decided to use people, just the way a sculptor uses clay." But, as in the ancient tale, McLaren's statue finally assumed a life of its own. In court, the ultimate Sex Pistols issues were now being raised: Who is the artist, and who is the product: the spokesperson or the puppeteer, the actor or the entrepreneur?

SID VICIOUS IN *THE GREAT ROCK 'N' ROLL SWINDLE*, 1979–80.

MADAM BUTTERFLY VIDEO, 1984.

Unknowingly, the court was ruling on a sophisticated aesthetic-philosophical issue. Observing conventional common sense and a humanistic conception of art based on the prejudice that physical gesture takes precedence over intellectual premeditation, the judge reached a decision. He threw out the idea of the producer-as-artist, and, on the grounds of mismanagement, awarded the musicians the money.

8. THE ARTIST OF THE FUTURE

Early in this century, the Italian Futurists articulated a wish for art to break out of the shackles of objecthood. They proposed that artists eventually be replaced by orchestrators of artistic effects, individuals and groups who are involved in the world outside the academic confines of art. As Bruno Corradini and Emilio Settimelli wrote in their manifesto of March 1914, "the producer of artistic creativity must join the commercial organization which is the muscle of everyday life."

Prefiguring the Surrealists and Situationists, they suggested that "the combination of elements (drawn from experience) more or less dissimilar is the necessary and sufficient raw material for any intellectual creation" and that "every artist will be able to invent a new form of art" which could include "the chaotic, unaesthetic, and heedless mixing of all the arts already in existence, and all those which are and will be created by the inexhaustible will for renewal." Finally, such an art, they predicted, "would have as its immediate effect the definitive placing of the artist in society."[21]

Six years later, at the Nineteenth State Exhibition in Moscow, the artist Alexander Rodchenko issued a not dissimilar manifesto:

Non-objective art has left the museums. Non-objective art is the street itself, the squares, the towns and the whole world. The art of the future will not be the cozy decoration of family homes. It will be just as indispensible as 48-story skyscapers, mighty bridges, the wireless, aeronautics and submarines which will be transformed into art.

The art of Malcolm McLaren is so deeply and invisibly embedded in the popular culture of today that we have failed to see him as an artist. But his ideas are being emulated by hundreds of pop culture figures who follow him. Last year, *Rolling Stone*, a magazine that had conspicuously underplayed punk rock during the 1970s, cited the Sex Pistols' album as the second most popular album in rock history. (In the context of *Rolling Stone*'s agenda, the Sex Pistols are a "black" version of the band whose *Sgt. Peppers* album was number one: the Beatles.) A further example of McLaren's influence was when, three years after the release of *Duck Rock*, the singer-songwriter Paul Simon followed McLaren's tracks to South Africa to record an album with local black musicians. Admittedly, Simon's purpose was not the re-invention of rock and roll through an appropriation of its origins; his sights were set on the American news and entertainment arenas at a moment of mounting American opposition to apartheid. Yet, while *Duck Rock*'s musical and political innovations are still to be widely appreciated and understood, Simon has won a standing ovation in Hollywood for his humanitarianism.

Malcolm McLaren knows that the distribution of art in the post-Pop era is the secret to greatness, just as the town-planners who redesigned London's Oxford Street after the Gordon Riots knew that power lay in a web of invisible controls over the masses. Yet, since relocating to Los Angeles in 1985, McLaren has made Hollywood his prey. (And, in 1989 he is also tackling Broadway.) Hollywood may possibly be the stage for McLaren's ultimate disappearing act. Alternatively, it may be like the Clocktower in Venice in 1910, from which a fierce Marinetti, the founder of Futurism and avant-garde propaganda, cast down hundreds of handbills, which drifted down into the outstretched arms of the delighted, innocent, unsuspecting world below.

NOTES

1. Boy George, in conversation with the author, 1985. Unless otherwise noted, all quotations by McLaren are from conversations with the author. Contractual amounts cited are also McLaren's, are stated in *The Great Rock 'n' Roll Swindle*, or they have been provided by McLaren's unauthorized biographer, Craig Bromberg.

2. "Malcolm McLaren," Thames TV *South Bank Show*, London, 1984.

3. Paul Rambali, "How the West Was Won," *The Face*, London, June, 1983, p. 42.

4. *The Face*, London, December, 1982.

5. "Phantom of the Opera," *Melody Maker*, London, August 25, 1984, p. 26.

6. Julie Burchill, *Damaged Gods*, London, 1987, pp. 16–54.

7. For a discussion of "bricolage," see Dick Hebdige, *Subculture: The Meaning of Style*, London, 1979, pp. 102–6.

8. Jamie Reid and Jon Savage, *Up They Rise: The Incomplete Works of Jamie Reid*, London, 1987, p. 15.

9. In conversation with the author, February, 1985. See also, Paul Taylor, "Pop's Smoking Pistol," *Vogue*, New York, April, 1986, p. 88.

10. Jon Savage, interview with Vivienne Westwood, *The Face*, London, January, 1981, p. 25.

11. Timothy J. Clark, letter to the author, February 21, 1987.

12. *South Bank Show*, op cit.

13. "Malcolm Moves On," *Women's Wear Daily*, New York, March 26, 1985.

14. "Phantom of the Opera," op cit.

15. "Anarchy in the UK," screenplay, first draft, July, 1977.

16. Reid and Savage, op cit. p. 85.

17. Fred and Judy Vermorel, *Sex Pistols: The Inside Story*, London, 1987, p. 138.

18. McLaren, letter dated March 15, 1979.

19. Simon Frith and Howard Horne, *Art Into Pop*, London, 1987, p. 124.

20. Malcolm McLaren, "Pop Catalyst," *Over 21*, London, May, 1982, p. 101.

21. "Weights, Measures and Prices of Artistic Genius," *Futurismo & Futurismi*, Milan, 1986, pp. 568–570.

FROM *LET IT ROCK* TO *WORLD'S END* 430 KING'S ROAD

Jane Withers

In late 1976, Malcolm McLaren and Vivienne Westwood's shop at 430 King's Road was reincarnated under the banner *Seditionaries*. When the shop opened, with its opaque glass facade and small name plaque, it had a clinically neat appearance reminiscent of a dentist's office. The pristine front, however, didn't last long. Within weeks, the shop, its windows reinforced with a metal grill, boarded up and emblazoned with graffiti, looked more like a betting shop under seige. *Seditionaries*' fortified facade emerged as a visual record of punk's rise amid the regular clashes of warring youth factions that congregated in the World's End area on weekends.

The antagonism incited by *Seditionaries* and demonstrated by the defaced facade, the police raids on the premises, and the campaigns launched to enforce the shop's closure, all reveal the extent to which the small shop was popularly perceived by both its supporters and adversaries, subcultural and establishment alike, as the catalyst and symbolic bastion of the punk revolt. Such theatrics as surrounded punk's rebellious upsurge had not been seen on King's Road since the sartorial pyrotechnics of the 1960s.

Seditionaries was the fourth in line, and certainly the most notorious, of the series of shops opened by Malcolm McLaren, Vivienne Westwood and a steady stream of collaborators on the site of 430 King's Road. From the fifties revival promoted by *Let It Rock* and *Too Fast To Live Too Young To Die*, to *Sex* and *Seditionaries*, the laboratories of the punk revolt, to *World's End*, the stage for the voyage into romantic historicism (and the shop that is still the showcase for Westwood's work today), 430 King's Road operated on the frontline of cult style. According to McLaren, it provided "a playground for eccentricities to occur."[1] The history of 430 King's Road in the 1970s offers a significant perspective on the developments of youth culture in that decade, and tells the story of McLaren and Westwood's adventures in cult style—their search for a metaphor for revolt. The precedent for McLaren and Westwood's venture into shopkeeping was the idea of the pop boutique as it had evolved in the London of the fifties and sixties—an environment McLaren and Westwood knew well.

The network of boutiques that emerged in London in the late fifties and early sixties provided an infrastructure for the rise of pop culture, transforming whole districts of London (King's Road and Carnaby Street were the main "boutique strips") into playgrounds for Mod consumption. They established the central role of the boutique as a forum for the assimilation and dissemination of subcultural style—a hothouse for cult activity. Shops like Mary Quant's *Bazaar* opened on the King's Road in 1955. Widely acknowledged as the first of the new boutiques, *Bazaar* spearheaded the post-war retail revolution. Displays were designed to shock, Quant recalls, creating an atmosphere of "a sort of permanently running cocktail party."[2] *Bazaar* and its followers re-invented fashion as fun, and shopping as a form of entertainment.

The "long front" of pop culture, as Lawrence Alloway described it, abolished traditional hierarchies of culture, value and taste, and promoted cultural convergence. The boutique played a cathartic role by providing a stage for pop culture's characteristic synthesis of the mutually sustaining iconographies of Pop Art, pop music, and pop fashions. For an emergent generation of artistic activators, the boutique environment presented a vehicle for effecting the artist's transfer, as Marshall McLuhan observed, from "the ivory tower to the control tower of society."[3]

Extravagant boutique designs dominated the landscape of the so-called "Swinging Sixties." Shops like *Granny Takes A Trip*, the psychedelic cavern on the King's Road that sold all the Hippie accoutrements for the "Summer of Love" and which once had an American car decorating its facade, provided a constant spectacle for the Saturday parade that frequented the strip. In many ways, these were pop culture's most flamboyant monuments. The pop boutique, as it evolved in the sixties, offered the possibility of an environment that was both an artistic and a commercial outlet—a fusion of studio and gallery, court and stage. To McLaren, who had spent a good part of the sixties in art school, "[The shop] was a replacement for being an artist in another way. You didn't want to paint pictures in 1970. You'd come out of the whole environmental school of thinking, that whole conceptual art."

It was this style of shopkeeping and movement-making, as well as the fading energy of the late Hippie era, that McLaren and Westwood revived and developed, making 430 King's Road the most singular and significant cult landmark of its time. If, as George Melly observed, Mary Quant's *Bazaar* contained "the embryonic concept of 'Swinging London,'" the series of shops initiated by McLaren and Westwood at 430 King's Road (*Sex* and *Seditionaries* in particular) played an equivalent role in the radically different subcultural subterfuges of the seventies.[4]

Situated way down the King's Road from Sloane Square, where the road bends round into Chelsea's more dilapidated area of World's End, 430 King's Road

WESTWOOD AND MCLAREN IN *LET IT ROCK*, 1972.

already had quite a track record in 1971 when McLaren and Westwood moved in. Its most recent incarnation was as *Mr. Freedom*, Tommy Robert's shrine to pop culture. *Paradise Garage* succeeded *Mr. Freedom* and capitalized on the rock 'n' roll revival, selling used denims and Americana behind what looked like a set for a desert gas station. It was this shop that most interested McLaren, providing as it did a timely foil to his own interest in the Teddy Boy cult.

McLaren and Westwood rented part of *Paradise Garage* and began by experimenting with styles of the fifties, promoting first the Teddy Boy and later the Rocker/Biker styles—archetypal images of the teenage rebel and synonymous with the heroic era of rock 'n' roll. The retro styles stood out in sharp contrast to the fading Hippie dress of the time—an ethos McLaren professed to hating.

Their *Let It Rock* was conceived as a shrine to the twin linchpins of Ted culture: music and sartorial style. Decorated as a faithful replica of a Ted's dream sitting room circa 1955, complete with a glass cocktail cabinet displaying period ornaments and accessories, guitar-shaped mirrors, cinema posters and framed photographs of rock 'n' roll idols, the shop provided an authentic backdrop for McLaren's collection of period records and music and cinema ephemera, and Westwood's flamboyant copies of Ted drape suits that made up the stock. The choice of a living room as the setting for the Ted revival reflected the urban, territorial nature of the Ted tribes. The living room was the symbolic proscenium for urban adventure, a style capsule that transported kids from the drab realities of daily life to the fantasy land of exaggerated style that Ted inhabited. With the jukebox blaring, the shop generated a club atmosphere and attracted a following of hardcore Teds and obsessive revivalists.

When *Paradise Garage* folded, McLaren took over the whole premises. The expanded *Let It Rock* had its name emblazoned on the facade in fluorescent letters stylized to look like musical notes. Inside the shop, the period flavor evolved into something reminiscent of a musical set with its black interior decorated with fifties posters and, as McLaren remembers, a scenic mural of "a lampost down a mean, dark Northern street at night in the fifties with smoke stacks in the background and a few posters."

McLaren used the space as a platform for fantastic displays created from bizarre ensembles of "found" props, clothing, and cult objects: T-shirts emblazoned with glitter names cascading down a ladder, a display of re-conditioned valve radios or a wall hung with chicken wire and used to display stiletto-heeled shoes. Westwood recalls those days:

Every Friday I used to be up all night sewing—making something for this special shop, painting the backs of leather jackets and putting studs on things and he'd be in there redecorating the shop. He'd be up all night redoing it as if it were an environmental happening each week. The shop was supposed to open about 10:30 - 11:00. By one o'clock he still wouldn't be finished and there'd be all these Teddy Boys outside the door saying, "come on Malcolm, let us in," and he wouldn't let them in until he'd finished.[5]

The transition in 1973 to *Too Fast To Live Too Young To Die* confirmed McLaren's shifting allegiance from the Teddy Boy to the Rocker style. The shop was given a new black fascia dominated by the new name (a slogan adopted by James Dean fans after his death) inscribed around a skull and cross-bones in the style of the emblems decorating Bikers' jackets. The stock changed too. Alongside the drapes and zoot suits were leathers and T-shirts extravagantly customized with studs, rips, zips, chains, even segments of bike tires—clothing inspired, according to Westwood, by the dress of the gangs of Bikers who congregated around Chelsea Bridge at the time.

The threatening machismo of the outlaw biker identity, charged by its associations with speed and danger and the spectre of death, provided a sinister counterpoint to the peacock pyrotechnics of the Teddy Boy. The switch to a less overtly retro idiom was tactical. McLaren and Westwood encountered the predicament of most ardent revivalists: the material culture may be easy enough to exhume, but the spirit is harder to resuscitate. The Ted revival, as Westwood explains, was stillborn: "Malcolm began to get bored with the ideas of Teddy boys basically. They just looked so amazing that he thought they were some kind of expression of revolt, and he just got rather tired in the end of them all talking about which record had come out on the same label."

As the disastrous social and economic conditions of the sixties became apparent, a widespread nostalgia focused on the seemingly more benign post-war decade of the fifties, whose imagery was absorbed into the mainstream and, in the process, divested of its power. A sanitized version of the Teddy Boy assumed an almost folkloric flavor as it took its place in the character repertoire of television and cinema. 430 King's Road was frequented by wardrobe departments searching out Ted dress for MOR TV popster Lionel Blair or period flavor for the David Essex rock revival movies *That'll Be The Day* and *Stardust*.

The compounded effect of all this was to convince McLaren to change tack, to forgo retro and embark on something new. The fetish element apparent in the Biker clothing was made the subject of the next adventure. When 430 King's Road re-opened in 1974, the intention was obvious: the new name, *Sex*, was emblazoned across the facade in giant shocking-pink letters.

The cult style of *Sex* was constructed from the iconography of the taboo. Raiding darkened closets, McLaren and Westwood flaunted their findings in public. The shop promoted hardcore rubber and leather, fetish and bondage wear as "alternative" streetwear, precipitating a demonic parade of the loaded and sterotypical images of sexual "perversity." As Westwood explained: "We were writing on the walls of the Establishment, and if there is one thing that frightens the Establishment, it's sex. Religion you can knock, but sex gives them the horrors."[6]

Sex was designed to amplify the subversive intent. Conceived as a parody of a conventional sex shop, its appearance mimicked the sleazy look of "authentic" sex shops—the kind secreted in red-light districts. The loud black and pink facade set the tone, and behind the shop name was sprayed the slogan, "Craft must have clothes but truth loves to go naked." The windows were boxed in like

SEX SHOP EXTERIOR, 1975.

SEDITIONARIES INTERIOR, 1977.

the display cases that offer a titillating glimpse of the wares inside a "real" sex shop. But in place of the usual pin-ups and fetish objects were *Sex* cult objects —studded jackets and customized T-shirts displayed against flesh-colored sponge. The central doorway was curtained to conceal the interior from public inquisition. It was deliberately intimidating.

Inside, the walls were lined with grey sponge and sprayed with pornographic and revolutionary slogans extracted from the writings of Alex Trocchi, who had become a conduit for the anarchistic philosophy of the International Situationists in the sixties. The bondage wear was displayed on mannequin torsos and hung on gym-like wall bars. The compounded effect created a dark and dangerous looking interior that drew vicarious energy from its apparent associations with a fetishist's torture chamber. The blaze of graffiti amplified the subversive nature of the enterprise, exploiting its associations as both the graphic style of protest and the illicit language of pornography scrawled in toilets.

Sex acted as a magnet drawing collaborators to the cause. The customers divided into two factions, as McLaren recalls:

Half were MPs and fetish buyers from out in the country places, from all over. And half were kids that came to the shop because it was so extraordinary. It suddenly swept them up and made them feel very dangerous and unique and important. It was a great ladder to climb, that shop. It was something that when kids had finally sequestered themselves into that environment they never wanted to leave.

Besides the intricate displays of hardcore fetish wear drawn from or inspired by the catalogues of specialist outfitters, the shop began to sell other clothes, like T-shirts decorated with porn images and revolutionary slogans. The famous bondage trousers were also developed under *Sex*'s reign. The effect of *Sex* clothing when paraded in public was predictably volatile. One man, David Fullbrook, was arrested on the King's Road for wearing the notorious T-shirt displaying two naked cowboys. The police raided the shop and McLaren and Westwood went to court, having hit on a style that provoked a direct confrontation with conservative British society. "If you want to find out how much freedom you really have," Westwood observed, "try making an extreme sexual statement in public."[7]

The *Sex* shop exemplifies the significant role of the cult shop in the development of subcultural style. As McLaren explains:

The environment of the shop gave the clothes a reason to exist because outside of that shop they may have looked a little less dangerous. They may have looked like where they had come from. The fifties clothes may have looked just like part of some old rubbish bin. The fetish clothes may have looked just like something you might have found if you'd crept into the backstreets of Richmond in some strange, backwater fetish shop. You put them into a position where suddenly they were culturally significant and they embodied another buzzword which was "Pop". They were pop everytime.

The success of *Sex* and the cult style it promoted was reliant on a dialogue. Operating at street level, the shop functioned as a forum for the assimilation and dissemination of ideas—a focus for an internal drama promoting a sense of a continuous narrative essential to subculture's existence. The shop had a paradoxical identity as both a covert, insular world, and as an outward challenge to society's values.

When punk exploded on the public horizon, it was time for another change: the shop was transformed into *Seditionaries*. If the seeds of iconographic subversion central to the punk revolt were nurtured in *Sex*'s exploration of the forbidden, *Seditionaries* expanded that lead into a new realm. *Seditionaries* was designed as a stage for punk's anarchic celebration of chaos and destruction as creative principles. Articu-

DAVID CONNOR SKETCH.

WORLD'S END SHOP FRONT, 1980.

PIRATE OUTFIT, 1981.

lating the inchoate nihilism of the punk revolt, *Seditionaries* presented a vision of an apocalyptic utopia that sought to locate punk on the precipice of cultural collapse.

While *Seditionaries'* facade with its metal-clad windows appeared symbolically fortified, the interior conjured up a disturbing innerworld haunted by the specter of violent destruction, past and future. The side walls were papered with vast black-and-white photographs of bomb-damaged Dresden in the aftermath of World War II and were illuminated by the glare of film lights protruding from a jagged hole in the ceiling. All this served to mediate and politicize the image of punk's own world-vision enshrined on the back wall: a vast color photograph of the most durable emblem of tourist London, Piccadilly Circus, inverted (an idea inspired by the fact that it is illegal to stick a postage stamp of the Queen's head upside down), to symbolize punk's own anarchic ambition to turn the world upside-down.

Seditionaries sold the staples of the punk uniform—bondage jackets and trousers, parachute jackets, long-sleeved "Anarchy" shirts and T-shirts decorated with porn images and political signifiers—all under the label "Clothes for Heroes," a legend also inscribed on the shop door. The media tag that

Seditionaries accrued as "couture" punk, and the relatively high prices of the clothing, reveal *Seditionaries'* status within the movement as something approaching a designer shop.

Despite the "Do-It-Yourself" ethos promoted by the eclectic punk style and the lip-service paid to the rejection of capitalism (a position for which McLaren and Westwood as shop owners were heavily criticized), punk precipitated a revival of alternative fashion outlets in London and the north of England on a scale that had not been seen since the sixties. For instance, another key King's Road shop, Stephane Raynor's *Boy*, shot to notoriety with its arsonist window display. Characteristic of punk's fetishism of violence and body mutilation, it comprised glass display cases containing bits of burnt clothing and what purported to be fragments of a corpse—the remains of an arsonist said to have been trapped in the shop after starting a fire. The effect of the mutilated limbs, made from a material that its creators, Peter Christoferson and John Harwood, called Revultex, was realistic enough for the police to carry out forensic tests and to fine the store for "Indecent Exhibition."

Boy's survival today as a thriving business that sells punk classics demonstrates how punk style has been incorporated into the vernacular. Cleansed of its original resonance, punk dress (much like new wave graphics) exists as simply another available style option in the ever-expanding pluralism of the late 1980s.

The final incarnation of 430 King's Road was *World's End*, named after its locale, thereby demonstrating the extent to which the shop had become a tourist attraction in its own right. This was Westwood and McLaren's last joint venture before their partnership broke up after almost a decade of experimenting with the "untouchable." Westwood and McLaren opened the eighties with their theatrical Pirates collection (as promoted by Adam Ant and Bow Wow Wow)—the first stop on a voyage picking through history and remote cultures in search of other images of the outlaw to succeed punk.

The design of *World's End* set the stage for an imaginative leap into a timeless world inspired by Alice's voyage through the Looking Glass, and is demarcated by the thirteen-houred clock that dominates the shop's cottage-style and bay-windowed facade. As if in fulfillment of the invocation of Alice's duchess, this world does go round "a deal faster than it does." But the clock's hands whirr backwards into a lost kingdom where the fantasies drawn out in the rich pageant of the clothing collide in an historical and cultural abyss.

Architect David Connor's series of drawings for the facade illustrate a collage of fairytale themes: Lewis Carroll's vision of the fantastic, fused with the crooked house of the Crooked Man, a pirate's galleon, and the chalet style of the cuckoo clock. The interior of the shop, its sloping wooden floor and chandelier with gold light bulbs illuminating the procession of mannequins used to display the current tribal identities, fulfills the promise of a magical half-world.

The idea of moving backwards through history and across cultural boundaries was presented in the design of *Nostalgia of Mud*, the shop McLaren and Westwood occupied for a brief period in St. Christopher's Place. The mud map which camouflaged the facade of the shop located the action somewhere in the sub-continent, and the design of the interior was inspired by the idea of an archaeological dig. The entrance level, hung with portraits and a giant chandelier, was partly cut away to reveal a bubbling pool in the mud-baked basement, a crumbling world layered to reveal its own past, stretching back from a pseudo-classical grandeur to primitive origins.

Although the flamboyant romanticism of Westwood's later collections, with their characteristically rich embroidery of color and style, appeared as the antithesis of the aggressively urban punk style, the most vital of punk's traits were continued. The elements collaged in punk's violent, cut-up dress style were often scavenged from the street or garbage can, symbolizing punk's emergence as a specter clothed in the detritus of society. The swaggering Pirates, the demonic Savages, the Hobos, the Witches and the Buffalos were punk's flamboyant successors, renewing the metaphor of the scavenger hero, the outlaw existing on the edge of society and feeding off it by encroaching on new territories. Tribal prints substituted for bondage. After punk's apocalypse, the spoils were the riches of the world, ideologically and culturally plundered from the history of the West and "Third World" and set magnificently in the modern city.

In the early *World's End* collections, Westwood carried over ideas from the punk movement into the mainstream. She effected the transfer begun with *Seditionaries* from the urban underground to the international fashion arena, reinforcing her continuing status as one of the most vital forces in contemporary fashion.

After a decade of post-punk, Westwood's 1987 distortions of British style, loaded with ironic references to a more glorious past and emblems of royalty (and Westwood's own public appearances

NOSTALGIA OF MUD SHOP FRONT, 1982.

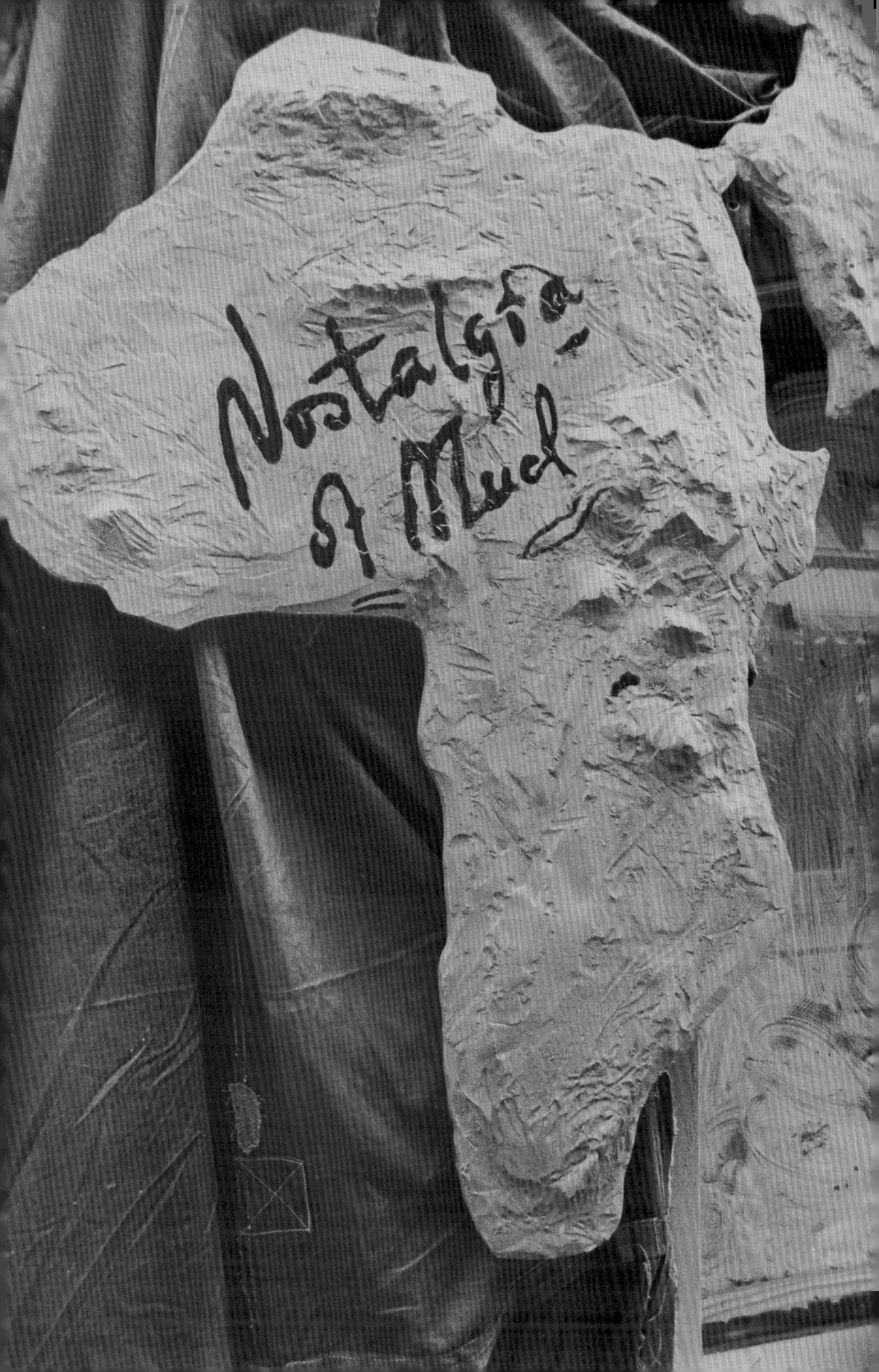

sporting an ersatz crown), are an ironic echo of Punk's inflammatory contribution to the Queen's 1977 Jubilee and the upheaval it caused—the Sex Pistols' "God Save The Queen," Jamie Reid's graphic of the Queen adorned with a safety-pin, and *Seditionaries* clothing. From radical protest to ironic emulation, the clothes fulfill, momentarily at least, Westwood's aim "to make the poor look rich and the rich look poor."[8]

The overwhelming effect of the eighties boom in retail design (something akin to the growth of advertising in the fifties and sixties—design is now offered as a palliative to relieve all ills) is evident in the current soulless confusion of styles and eras. Design styles are plundered and their currency rapidly undermined by hollow replication in the mainstream. One example is the stark minimalism pioneered in shop design by the new wave of Japanese fashion designers. Today, a watered down version of that style is widely deployed by the mass-market fashion chains.

The whole idea of style-oriented retail initiated by the boutique and central to subculture's existence, the idea of creating a complete environment that embodies the message and essence of the fashion image, has been adopted as a mainstream fashion marketing technique. Like fashion itself, the shop environment evokes a lifestyle image and offers the promise of transformation.

In a culture polarized by visions of wealth and the grim urban reality of a less glorious Britain, escapism has become a national pastime. Style culture has been abbreviated to lifestyle consumerism, and shop design annexed to the accelerating cycle of consumption and disposal central to fashion and on which the modern economy is reliant.

The evolution of 430 King's Road in the seventies and eighties reveals the rejuvenating role of the shop for cult style and its place as a landmark in avant-garde design—an artist's studio for the fermentation of new ideas.

NOTES

1. All quotations by Malcolm McLaren are from an interview with the author, October, 1986.

2. Mary Quant, Quant by Quant, London, 1966, p. 45.

3. Marshall McLuhan, "Understanding Media," Quoted by Robert Hewison, Too Much: Art and Society in the Sixties, 1960-75, London, 1986, p. 48.

4. George Melly, Revolt into Style, London, 1970, p. 147.

5. All quotations by Vivienne Westwood, unless otherwise noted, are from an interview with the author, November, 1986.

6. Vivienne Westwood, quoted in Fashion Guide, London, 1978, p. 164.

7. Ibid.

8. Vivienne Westwood, interviewed in "The Shock of the New" by Georgina Howell, The Times, London, August 23, 1983.

THE GREAT ROCK 'N' ROLL SWINDLE
Jon Savage

> *All cities are geological: you cannot take three steps without encountering ghosts bearing all the prestige of their legends. We move within a closed landscape whose landmarks constantly draw us toward the past. Certain shifting angles, certain receding perspectives, allow us to glimpse original conceptions of space, but this vision remains fragmentary. It must be sought in the magical locales of fairy tales and surrealist writings: castles, endless walls, little forgotten bards, mammoth caverns, casino mirrors.*
>
> Ivan Chtcheglov, 1953

•

This starts as a London story. One beginning (and there are as many as there are participants in this collective work) can be found in the "Oxford Street" film project that Malcolm McLaren worked on when attending Goldsmiths' College in 1969. A short film about the past and the present of one of London's central thoroughfares, it was an attempt at a practical psychogeography. McLaren was fascinated by the way in which Oxford Street, a pure shopping environment, worked: the cheap, quickly changing facades, the harsh lighting in the hamburger joints to make you vacate your seat more quickly, the tawdry, mass-produced standard of the goods and services on offer. The film was never completed, but it included interviews, done by McLaren himself, with a Wimpy Bar designer, with various employees of the big department store Selfridges (the site of a Situationist happening some years later, where "assistants" handed out goods free) and with singer Gene Vincent and archetypal English androgyne rocker Billy Fury.

In this unpromising psychic environment, McLaren and Vivienne Westwood initially practiced a sharper version of the already ubiquitous retro styles: they did 1950s instead of 1930s, Teddy Boys instead of Gangsters. In contrast to the quick turnover, Oxford Street approach of the typical King's Road boutiques, *Let It Rock*, as the shop was called, was designed like a fifties living room. It became a hang-out for obsessives, selling new versions of the Edwardian drapes that, in the hands of working-class youth, had transformed London's landscape from 1953 on and, later, the Rocker or Biker clothing—leathers, studs, fetish—that did the same to Britain's roads from the late fifties. As Jeff Nuttall wrote, "There was something satisfying about the way in which a traffic stream on a hot Saturday, stalled, crammed with sweaty pink families trapped with one another as the Mini-Minor was trapped in the queue, could be utterly *negated*, cancelled, by a group of gleaming rockers hurtling past."[1] Although Westwood and McLaren provided costumes for films such as *That'll Be The Day* and Ken Russell's *Mahler*, they were slowly getting bored.

As the macho conservatism of the Teddy-Boy revivalists became more and more apparent, the pop-culture archives were looted even deeper into the American zoot suit, and the shop's name changed to *Too Fast To Live Too Young To Die*. Skull and crossbones were displayed on the shop front; peg pants, extravagant jackets, and lurid ties were inside. One, in green, brown and beige, tells a story: a couple eat, hold each other and then mount the stairs, the legend reads: "And so to bed." Soon, however, Westwood and McLaren hit the blank wall that all sellers of second-hand styles run into—the need for something new, not used. The novelty was "sex." As Westwood said later in an interview with sex-manual magazine *Forum*, "We're not here to sell toys and fetish clothing but to *convert*, *educate* and *liberate*. We're totally committed to what we're doing and our message is simple. We want you to live out your wildest fantasies to the hilt."[2] Out Of The Bedroom And Into The Streets: here, according to Wilhelm Reich, is one key to the door of Western oppression, nowhere more so than in Britain, that most closeted of countries where the most fundamental scandals are always sexual.

•

Yes. Sex is the only way to infuriate them. Much more fucking and they'll be screaming hysterics in no time.
Joe Orton, 1967

There is only collage, cutting and splicing. This explains fairly well what Jean-François Lyotard calls the disappearance of the great narratives. Classless society, social justice—no-one believes in them any more. We're in the age of micro-narratives, the art of the fragment. I believe only in the collage: it's trans-historical.
Paul Virilio, *Pure War*, 1983

Much of the original collection of *Sex* was seriously consumed by genuine users of the clothing, i.e. fetishists, sadomasochists, etc. This was deliberate. The rubber T-shirts, skirts, the "Thongs" of Alex Trocchi's 1969 novel, the masks—displayed on a wooden bar on the wall as if in a gym—were all fit for display in *Atomage*, the rubber specialists' magazine. (McLaren had visited the magazine's owner in Covent Garden just to make sure.) Yet as before, the restrictions of a specialist interest became apparent: the perverts were a bit pink, dull and closeted. Fired by the example of women like Jordan (Pamela Rooke from Seaford), who wore the clothing on the commuter train from Brighton (thus reminding the businessmen all too clearly of their hidden leisure moments), and Linda, who had to wear the clothing to work and was thrilled because she didn't need to change to go outside anymore, Westwood decided to go for something more expansive.

Some original T-shirts were made: a square of cloth, with holes slashed at

ALBUM COVER, 1974.

neck and arms (and, sometimes, at the nipples, with added zips) which bear images from gay or pedophilic magazines, quotes from Alex Trocchi's *School For Wives* porn novel, false breasts or other provocative material. One, "You're Gonna Wake Up One Morning and Know What Side Of The Bed You've Been Lying On!" was designed by printer Bernard Rhodes (Clash manager, 1977-78, 1983-85) as a manifesto for the new age. The power of this clothing was demonstrated by the arrest of one customer in July 1975 for wearing the "Cowboy Cocks" T-shirt as he passed through Piccadilly Circus: its legend spoke of boredom—"Ello Joe Been anywhere lately Nah, its all played aht Bill, Getting to [sic] straight."

A space was beginning to open up. The fetish clothing became a fashion item—as opposed to a practical accoutrement. A slogan spray-painted on the wall read: "What matters is to jump out of the suburbs as fast as you possibly can." At the same time, explains Jordan, the shop's infamous assistant, the clientele changed:

On one side of the shop we'd have all this stuff laid out for the rubber men—that's what we'd call the guys that would just come in and buy the rubber gear—and on the other side we'd have the beginnings of all the punk stuff. They were always very quiet and, being used to buying mail order, they weren't used to

MCLAREN WITH BERNIE RHODES AND DOLLS MANAGER MARTIE THAU.

going in a shop and buying it. They didn't like the punks being in the same shop at all.

Other clothing was added to the line: turquoise forties "flasher" raincoats, leather trousers, and what became known as the "Anarchy" shirt, a striped 60's Wemblex (or equivalent raw material) silk-screened in various colors and adorned with patches of cloth with a jumble of explicit political signifiers, such as pictures of Karl Marx or small swastikas, and slogans taken from Situationist and late sixties' libertarian politics. "A Bas Le Coca Cola," "Be Reasonable: Demand The Impossible," "Only Anarchists Are Pretty."

●

The phenomenon exploded in some four million viewer's eyes. Suddenly, as if catapulted from top-secret rocket installations, Johnny and his men charged. Broke through the security veneer. Gained the stage. Johnny sensed the magic of being in front of an audience. On stage. He charged forward, sent Bobby Sharp flying as he grabbed the mike. He swung, saw his "Jolly Green Men" take care of their instrumental opposites. He glowed. This was it....

Richard Allen, *Teeny Bopper Idol*, 1973

Encouraged by kids like ex-skinhead Steve Jones and budding art student Glen Matlock, who came to avail themselves of the shop's open space, McLaren decided that the *Sex* shop needed a Sex band. Something like a mutant Bay City Rollers, then a massively popular teenscream group manipulated, in the classic tradition, by a homosexual manager, or a London New York Dolls. McLaren had a name—"QT Jones and the Sex Pistols"—that unconsciously echoed the aggressive hippiedom of his founding politics in the late sixties. But the new group wasn't up to much—floundering through versions of Faces' songs and Bad Company's "Can't Get Enough." With Warwick Nightingale, Glen Matlock, Paul Cook and Steve Jones as singer they rehearsed for a year without much success. They needed a focus. Vivienne Westwood and Bernard Rhodes had noticed three youths, all called John, who came into *Sex* regularly to pose. The most striking was John Beverley (who later became infamous as Sid Vicious), but he disappeared at the crucial moment. The choice alighted on John Lydon, who, encouraged by his friend John Grey, passed an "audition" by singing along to Alice Cooper's teen-angst classic "18." He was given the 1975 equivalent of a Pop Art pop name: Johnny Rotten.

Ten years and two bitter court actions later, it's clear that McLaren and Westwood were in possession of the situation, the ideas, the package, the space, but that, above anybody, John Lydon himself turned "hype" into "culture." With John Lydon (and perhaps this is what McLaren and those involved recognized) we enter a world of the archetype, of the slightly touched, demonic harbinger of destruction and disorder, a conflation of Dickens characters—Oliver Twist, Sim Tappertit, Abiezer Coppe, the title character from *Barnaby Rudge*, who foretold of an apocalyptic collapse of values and delivered utopian heresies with a scourging moral authority, or the 17-year-old revolutionary Steerpike, described in *Titus Groan*:

His body has the appearance of being malformed, but it would be difficult to say what gave it this gibbous quality. Limb by limb it appeared that he was sound enough, but the sum of these several members accrued to an unexpectedly twisted total. His face was pale like clay and save for his eyes, masklike. These eyes were set very close together, and were small, dark red, and of startling concentration.

•

We have a world of pleasures to win, and nothing to lose but boredom.
Raoul Vaneigem, "A Toast to Revolutionary Workers," 1972

"Actually, we're not into music," one of the Pistols confided afterwards. What then? *"We're into chaos."*
Neil Spencer, first Sex Pistols review, *New Music Express*, 1976

With the finally constituted Sex Pistols, McLaren tried to infiltrate the music industry. The group constantly bickered and fell apart weekly. In this late hippie era, no one took them seriously, but at least this created a bond. They began to gatecrash concerts and posed as the opening group at colleges: "What do you mean you don't know who we are? You *booked* us!" They played the "pub rock" circuit of small London venues, but found them unsuitable for their growing fury and the extravagant behavior of their "pan-sexual" fans. Their appearance was extraordinary: *Sex* clothes were mixed with the shop's remaining stock of past youth subcultural styles (Mod, Ted, Skinhead, Spiv, Rocker) and were put together with safety-pins in inspired collage. The "authorship" of the safety pin device is variously claimed by or on behalf of Jordan, Jackie Curtis, Richard Hell, Sid Vicious, and John Lydon, and is so confused as to make it a collective project. In this way, the "history" of youth culture was cut and spliced into fragments. Yet this was no mere postmodernist project: the four members of the group—particularly Jones and Lydon—infused these clothes (in the context of the time, a mix of the two then warring teen factions, Skin and Glam) with a real sense of underclass menace.

This collaging was also reflected in the group's handbill designs by Helen Wellington-Lloyd (a contemporary of

MCLAREN AND ORIGINAL SEX PISTOLS AT EMI CONTRACT SIGNING, 1976.

McLaren's at Goldsmiths' College) and Jamie Reid. Wellington-Lloyd began with a basic graphic style born out of poverty, speed and expediency, using torn photos, hand lettering and basic black-and-white printing. Using his printing expertise and the style he had developed with the Suburban Press, Jamie Reid took this style further, featuring "ransom note" lettering cut out from newspaper headlines—the mass media's curse negated—put together with crudely chopped, unrecognizable pictures of the group and obscure slogans, printed roughly in black and white—like secret communiques in an occupied country. This became the dominant punk aesthetic and its fragments are still ubiquitous.

MCLAREN AND THE SEX PISTOLS
AT THE A & M PRESS CONFERENCE, 1977.

Musically, the Sex Pistols synthesized various elements from the sixties and the seventies. Despite being presented as a radical break, it was cobbled together from tough London mod music—the Small Faces, early era Who—and riffs stolen from Glam rockers like Mud and renegade hippies like Hawkwind. What was "new," in the stifling summer of 1976, was Rotten's moral authority, worthy of Abiezer Coppe, the extraordinary behavior, the splendor of their small group of dedicated followers, and the collective depth of information that went into their creation. All of this enabled the Sex Pistols to crash through barrier after barrier as they slowly woke up to the extent of their power.

SINGLE COVER, DESIGN BY JAMIE REID, 1977.

What are the politics of boredom?
Malcolm McLaren, slogan for the
New York Dolls, 1974

Just as Westwood's bondage suit—unveiled by John Lydon at the Chalet Du Lac, Paris, in September 1976—epitomized both the physical and psychic restraints of modern life and the commitment necessary to overcome those restraints, the phrase "Boredom" described the expansive, occluded, utopian politics that built up at the Sex Pistols' core. This was derived not from theoretical Situationism but Situationism at the point of action, not from the incessant bickering between Guy Debord and the excluded; not the often badly translated and distributed texts, but from the slogans and events that caught the mood of possibility in Paris, May 1968—a brief glimpse of freedom sparked by Situationist activity and much romanticized thereafter. This world view had only reached England in small doses—tiny magazines like *King Mob* or *Fire*, hidden in the communiques of the UK terrorists the Angry Brigade, or popularized by Richard Neville's hippie potboiler, *Play Power* (1970). But everyone involved with the Sex Pistols instinctively realized Boredom's spatial aspect and used its rhetoric as a key.

The conduit, as it should be, was the media. Early in 1979, in the last days of the Sex Pistols, Malcolm McLaren and Jamie Reid wrote as clear a statement of past intention as one would ever get, on the back of the "Something Else" 45 sleeve. "The media was our lover and helper and that in effect was the Sex Pistols' success. As today to control the media is to have the power of Government, God or both." Just as the Situationists had first described the media totality that was to become a postmodernist commonplace, a highly developed sense of media politics and media terrorism was implanted in the Sex Pistols from the beginning: whether from McLaren's own considerable talents as a provocateur, Jamie Reid's knowledge of Fleet Street (passed on from his father who was an editor), Steve Jones' extreme recklessness, or Lydon's devastating quotes and song lyrics.

On the first of December 1976, the curses contained in a song like "I Wanna Be Me"—"I got you in my camera/I got you in my camera/A second of your life/Ruined for life"—came to pass, as the Sex Pistols swore at intoxicated TV host Bill Grundy and, more shockingly, ignored the unwritten laws of television etiquette. Within a few minutes, they became national and international news. Initially confused, McLaren moved very quickly to turn the situation to his own advantage. In a TV clip from the time, McLaren is shown sitting in close-up, in front of quiet Sex Pistols who look like naughty schoolboys hauled up before the headmaster. He's being quizzed about why the Sex Pistols won't speak to the press and why they are being prevented from fulfilling their performance commitments on their projected "Anarchy" tour. The interviewer begins with a typical, boring canard: "It's said that you're sick on stage, you spit at the audience and so on. I mean how can this be a good example to children?" McLaren totally ignores this tired discourse: "Well people are sick everywhere. People are sick and tired of this country telling them what to do." An abyss of possibility opened up.

•

They are Dickensian-like urchins who with ragged clothes and pock marked faces roam the streets of foggy gas-lit London pillaging. Setting fire to buildings. Beating up old people with gold chains. Fucking the rich up the arse. Causing havoc wherever they go. Some of these ragamuffin gangs jump on tables amidst the charred debris and with burning debris play rock 'n' roll to the screaming delight of the frenzied pissing pogoing mob. Shouting and spitting "anarchy" one of these gangs call themselves the SEX PISTOLS. This true and dirty tale has been continuing throughout 200 years of teenage anarchy and so in 1978 there still remains the SEX PISTOLS. Their active extremism is all they care about because that's WHAT COUNTS TO JUMP RIGHT OUT OF THE 20TH CENTURY AS FAST AS YOU possibly can in order to create an environment that you can TRUTHFULLY RUN WILD IN.

[signed] Oliver Twist
Malcolm McLaren, handbill/manifesto for the Sex Pistols, 1978

The cornerstones of McLaren's world were soft porn, Charles Dickens, Marx and the Bash Street kids. And when the band started, the main element was definitely the Bash Street kids. To the Sex Pistols, the record business looked like one giant slap up feed. The people in charge were either posh kids, fat kids or both. Now everybody knows that posh kids and fat kids always have the best toys. But all you have to do is trip them up once and they start to cry. That's what the Pistols did to the rock business in the very beginning: they made it cry.

John Varnom, 1979

The rest is history, of sorts, as it is and always was part of another, older, longer dialectic. The Sex Pistols fused Dickens with Debord, pulp author Richard Allen with Alex Trocchi, Spivs (English black marketeers) with Situationists—revealing hitherto unrecognized correspondences. In the weeks following the Grundy interview, the exploitative practices of the music industry became scrutinized as never before: "The Only

SEX SHOP T-SHIRTS, 1973–76.

Notes That Matter Are The Ones That Come In Wads," "Cash From Chaos" were some of the December 1976 tabloid headlines—later re-used in that anti-music industry tract *The Great Rock 'n' Roll Swindle*. In a memorable article, the *Daily Mail* printed a picture of EMI Managing Director Leslie Hill's £400,000 house (1976 prices, double or treble now) in Gerrards Cross, a deep suburb of London: the real power behind the industry was exposed. After *The Great Rock 'n' Roll Swindle*, the politics were removed from McLaren's parable by a generation of managers and hucksters after profit rather than possibility: the result was Spandau Ballet, Frankie Goes To Hollywood, and the attendant miseries of postmodernist pop.

In the decay of the postwar British consensus, a space was opened as quickly as it closed. It became possible to look at the world in a different way. A new map of London was imposed—a mixture of frantic, often subterranean movement as people felt empowered (celebrated in subway songs like "Day By Day," "Let's Submerge" and "Submission," as if the key was to be found in the endless tunnels of London's Underground), the black and white xeroxing of stark, inner urban images, the declamation of bitter, visionary lyrics and an extravagant, public display, which, with its deliberately baffling signals, gave a coded clue to this hyperactive motion.

The King's Road became a theater, which had not been seen since the sixties. Following the hidden subcultural references contained in the Sex Pistols and other groups, such as the Clash (whose handbills contained references to pulp classics like *Generation X* and sociological treatises like Stanley Cohen's *Folk Devils and Moral Panics*), it became the site of media fostered, pitched battles between punks and Teds, enraged at McLaren's "defection" from their cause. Here was the start of the "Style Wars," as described by Peter York in 1978, which have passed into world currency as a result of their unraveling through British pop music and pop videos.

The point of wearing punk or affiliated costume was to provoke, to incite, to take things out of the closet and into the streets, as Westwood well understood. In a monochrome urban environment, ten color electric mohair sweaters, bleached hair and all manner of leather and vinyl—ironically, just as had happened with the Edwardians in 1953—was as much a political annexing of space as it was the by now traditional right of those involved with youth culture to dress like peacocks. The locks and chains that emerged as a staple of punk costume were a theatrical expression of boredom's prison. This very novelty—of living in present time as opposed to Britain's perennial past—attracted na-

STILL FROM RUSS MEYER'S FOOTAGE FOR THE PROPOSED SEX PISTOLS FILM,
AS REPRODUCED ON *THE GREAT ROCK 'N' ROLL SWINDLE* SOUNDTRACK ALBUM, 1980.

SID VICIOUS COVER BY WARHOL,
ART & TEXT AND *FILE* MAGAZINES JOINT ISSUE, 1986.

tionwide hostility as well as wide attention. In the year of the Queen's Jubilee, Johnny Rotten appeared as her negative image on magazine covers the world over, just as Jordan uncannily resembled the rising political star, Margaret Thatcher. Punks became a negative tourist attraction. Today, the punks who congregate in the King's Road pose for tourist or postcard photographs, *Time* magazine covers, and resemble nothing so much as an up-to-date Beefeater, that cuddly piece of Britain's glorious past.

●

1976–77-81–78-82–79-83–80-77
78–79-80
86–76-86–77-77–78-79–80
76–81-82–83-77
78–79-80–79
86–76-86–76-86–76-77
77–77-77–78-77–78-80–1986

Strafe Für Rebellion, "Not For Radio," 1986

Punk nihilism is a modernist celebration of commodity fetishism: society's renovation of patriarchal rule. "He who fights the dragon becomes the dragon." (Nietzsche) Commodity madness, in its decadence and apathy, now breeds monsters as its gladiators to fight itself in the spectacle.

Catalyst Times, July, 1977

It's easy now to point to punk's weak spots, but this is to ignore the fact that its success was unexpected and catalytic. For a few months, many things seemed possible. The last two years, however, have seen the full recognition of punk's cooption. As Fredric Jameson writes, "the most offensive forms of . . . art—punk rock, say or what is called sexually explicit material—are all taken in stride by society, and they are commercially successful."[3] Yet the "retrospectives" that have dominated the British and American pop media since early 1986 illustrate the terms through which this has been negotiated. In August, 1987, the Sex Pistols' *Never Mind the Bollocks* appeared as number two on *Rolling Stone*'s "The 100 Best Albums Of The Last Twenty Years," its vision and complexities—and the historical moment to which it belonged—reduced to "the most exciting rock and roll record of the seventies." It's worth remembering, within the new multi-media industrial "integrated circuit," that the term "rock and roll" has a specific market connotation emphasized by the ads that framed the supplement—Reebok, Warner, Columbia, Mercury, House of Seagram, and Art Carved class rings.

Just as Alex Cox's film *Sid and Nancy* (1986) reduced a tragedy to a soap, recent accounts of punk have concentrated on it as music. The partial history recounted above shows that punk was much more, but that it foundered on its commercial peg: once involved with the music industry, the Sex Pistols' struggle was less with the outside world than with the industry itself. Much of this—following the success of "God Save The Queen," but especially after Lydon left the Sex Pistols in January 1978—had more to do with individual disputes than utopian politics. By 1978, punk was the avant-garde of late, consumer capitalism, and it functioned as a laboratory for a music business at the point of merging with the media industries in general. It provided young flesh in the form of a whole generation of musicians and an unprecedented sophistication in design and packaging. Single sleeves mutated into pop videos, and every significant new group arrived readymade, perfect for the postmodern age of information and consumption.

Malcolm McLaren has similarly been integrated, as much as is possible, into the obliterating visibility of the mainstream media. The ambitious Bow Wow Wow project—a mixture of clothes, politics and attitude as before—foundered on its very isolation of the music industry's weak spot: as "C30 C60 C90 GO!" encouraged home-taping and piracy (anticipating the Digital Audio Tape wars and the effect of sampling technology) EMI killed any chance it had of making the charts. *Duck Rock* was the first postmodern attempt at a new World Music. The "Buffalo Gals" single broke hip-hop commercially, and prepared Trevor Horn for his work with Frankie Goes To Hollywood.

"Soweto" helped pave the way for the situation where the Bhundu Boys open for Madonna in front of a 75,000 crowd. And then came *Fans*, and another album in 1988, film projects in Hollywood and regular talk show appearances in London. This might seem like a terrible diminuendo—McLaren as a kind of bright spot that the media can't rub out and likes to patronize—but it's not surprising. The hegemonic media industry—now the ideological wing that props up the West's domination—has learned the lessons of punk all too well. As Jordan observes: "You will never, ever again see such a culture gap." Culture is too important to capital for such an intervention to occur again.

Today, the London that McLaren and so many others helped to transform has returned to a better-scrubbed, but more sinister decay: the decay of thought, optimism and the wish to get to grips with present and future. Instead of punk's vaunting relish in monochrome, rips and spaces, there is the glaring brightness of the cheap, synthetic material that is now being used to paper over the cracks—like the plastic coping that covers beautiful Edwardian tiles in the "improved" Underground stations. In 1988, the most visible sign of London is reconstruction work and the youth culture most avidly sought after by advertisers and the magazines that are their handmaiden, the 25-year-old commodity brokers with their bengal striped shirts, paisley ties, red Porsches and cellular phones. This glaring exposure of commodities deliberately renders punk quaint and "old-fashioned" but provides its own solution: a new kind of invisibility. We are now twelve years away from the millenium and at present, it looks as though punk was its last rehearsal. The inheritors of punk's wish to transform the world are to be found, with patience, away from the media, away from its looped time and its insistence that everything must be brought to light. Outside the walls, the ragamuffin gangs that McLaren conjured up from the nightmare visions of Dickens and Hogarth still whirl like dervishes to break the dread spell of these times.

The Sex Pistols created a tremendous amount of debris, and that was very rewarding. It's like a child who loves to destroy something in order to find out what it's made of . . . smash everything . . . they just weren't able to construct anything from the debris. [But] that was just the beginning.

Malcolm McLaren,
Threepenny Review, 1983

NOTES

1. Jeff Nuttall, Bomb Culture, London, 1968.

2. Interview with Vivienne Westwood, Forum, June, 1976.

3. Fredric Jameson, "Postmodernism, or the Cultural Logic of Late Capitalism," New Left Review, 146, July-August, 1984.

MALCOLM MCLAREN
AND THE MAKING OF ANNABELLA

Dan Graham

BOW WOW WOW, 1981.

I'm 15 and a fool
Can't you see
So don't fall in love with me
I'm a rock and roll puppet in a band
* called Bow Wow Wow*
But I want to be a rabbit
At least they had more fun with a gun

I just go on and on and on
I'm supposed to sing that one
'Pop Pop gun'
And the Greeks had a word for it,
Went like this:
Chihuahua, Chihuahua

Bow Wow Wow, 1981

1. THE PRODUCER AS ARTIST

In 1980, Malcolm McLaren was asked by Adam and the Ants to reshape their image. His first move was to replace Adam with a new lead singer, a 14-year-old amateur singer of Burmese origin named Annabella Lwin. Guitarist Matthew Ashman saw McLaren as a kind of Moses-figure:

McLaren come along to be our manager for Adam and the Ants. And he told us kick Adam out. So we did. Adam was writing all the songs before McLaren come along, McLaren come along, separated Adam from the band and said "You're the band, you write the songs." We came up with this sound that we liked—because we'd all been listening to that music for a while as a band. And Adam wasn't very good really. Didn't really like him. He wasn't very good at dancing. Thought he was a bit old: he was 25. So, McLaren said 'kick him out.' So we said 'yeah, all right.' And we kicked him out and got her in.

McLaren is a typical product of the British art school system. At 42 years of age, he is from the generation caught between the radical movements of the late sixties (Paris '68 and the American counter-culture) as well as Pop and Conceptual Art's strategies for confronting mass, commercial culture. He is both a Pop artist and hippie entrepreneur. As a rock manager, he automatically follows in the footsteps of American discjockey Allen Freed, whose manipulation made rock 'n' roll a commercial form of music identified with white, urban, male teenage rebellion. His other predecessor is Brian Epstein, Liverpool record shop owner, intellectual businessman, but in McLaren's words, "a pathetic (homosexual) closet case." Both Freed and Epstein (like McLaren) were Jewish. Both had a perverse attraction for adolescent sexuality. Both appeared "revolutionary" in the way they exploited the media for their own purposes. Both men died tragically, victimized by the media in revenge for their earlier exploitation of it.

In 1974, McLaren went to New York and attempted to manage the New York Dolls: "I tried to turn them into something that could be a little . . . dangerous. The Vietnam war was about to end. I said . . . red was the color . . . let's use Mao and . . . the hammer and sickle . . . and use all the things that America right now is arrogant about and . . . make it an event." Applying this Situationist idea of public spectacle to the group's performances, he designed completely red outfits for the band who performed against a background of the hammer and sickle. After the Dolls had disbanded, McLaren, who had been influenced by the emerging New York City "punk rock" scene—the Ramones, Richard Hell and the Voidoids, Patti Smith—decided to apply the "punk" style to a more English, political context. He created the Sex Pistols out of "street people," non-musicians who hung about his boutique *Sex* on the King's Road, basing their early songs on the premise that rock is a means of defining a new class, one which Marx hadn't conceived of—youth.

Many of McLaren's ideas derive from Situationism, most obviously the notion that alienation has its roots in the problem of leisure-time and consumption rather than in the contradictions implicit within production. Another Situationist concept, that of the society as spectacle, influenced other key figures of the sixties, notably Abbie Hoffman, whose media-type radicalism was aimed at transforming the passivity of the hippies; Jean-Luc Godard, who used the interview form in *Le Gai Savoir* to examine the subversiveness of the youth as a class; and Andy Warhol, whose idea that in the future everyone will be famous for fifteen minutes, can be detected in McLaren's creation of anti-stars Johnny Rotten and Sid Vicious.

In the early 1950s, economic changes brought about a new category of consumer, the adolescent, and a new ideology, rock 'n' roll. No longer required after school as an entity within the increasingly automated, productive sphere, teenagers were, in effect, a new class with a huge buying power and little responsibility to the Protestant work-ethic of their elders. Then, as the concept of total leisure turned to boredom, teenagers' understanding of "freedom" led to revolt, or at least to pseudo-revolt. But adult society must be tolerant; the simple fact is that teenagers and rock music are essential to the economy.

Rock is the first musical form to be totally commercial and consumer-exploitative. It is largely produced by adults for the purpose of exploiting a vast adolescent market whose consciousness it manipulates through radio, film, magazines and television. The industry doesn't care if the message of rock is anarchistic or anti-society as long as it can make money from the music. Yet, at the same time, rock expresses the real ideology of adolescent culture. Although exploited, rock culture redefines the codes of music. Intermediaries from the adult world, such as Allan Freed, play an ambiguous role. On the one hand, he can be seen as a Moses-like, martyred prophet leading the teenagers toward a new musical religion; on the other, he can be viewed as an exploiter and profiteer who manipulated the desires of innocent youths.

Moreover, rock is the first commercial form of music which contains this self-conscious knowledge within its structure. Rock stars, who are both real adolescents and fictions of the entertainment world, become models for a new class which refuses to grow up—the myth of James Dean is exemplary. Taking momentary pleasures of the body to their limits transcends the forces of history and death. Pleasure is oblivion; there are no moral consequences. Death is a technique to achieve fame and eternity.

McLaren obviously saw the consequences of this "generation gap" as being potentially revolutionary, an inbuilt anarchistic mechanism to disrupt the system. Rock music, he said:

could change youth into becoming a continuous rebellion . . . If you're a manager of a rock 'n' roll band . . . you [can be] a hit and run provocateur of new political solutions within youth as a class and within media as such. . . . If you can divorce youth from its seniors . . . you have a new class [music] which can engineer a solution in which these kids can come together for the purpose of creating as much havoc as possible and changing their lives.

His analysis of youth as the leaders of a new society based on mass unemployment and total leisure, is contained in Bow Wow Wow's second single "W.O.R.K." This agit-prop "rap" sees "technology as the demolition of Daddy," the end of a form of society based on

BOW WOW WOW BOOKLET DESIGN BY NICK EGAN, 1981.

patriarchical subordination to "your parents . . . to your teacher . . . to your boss." McLaren used late sixties Yippie ideas and applied them to the current situation in Britain where the unemployed are provided with enough money to allow them to continue consuming. "You can't tell a kid who's 10 years old today that he may have a career when he reaches 18. That's old-fashioned because his old man who's 50 is probably redundant. . . . There should be bands on 'Top of the Pops' consisting of 50-year-old assembly line workers singing 'Ford Get Out. On We Go.'" With this in mind, McLaren tried to make a video for the song "W.O.R.K." which was to be shot in a Mini Metro plant "like Jean-Luc Godard. Very Maoistic, with all the robotic plants going around . . . with very big slogans like Godard used in *Made in the U.S.A.* saying 'DEMOLITION OF THE WORK ETHIC.'"

2. THE PRODUCTION OF DESIRE

I find sexuality in children a really potent way of them laying claims against this society. Sex, ultimately, as you know, is one of the most powerful selling forces in the world. It's something everybody cares about, and it has a lot of magic and a lot of taboos . . .

Malcolm McLaren

In the writing of Herbert Marcuse, American "counterculture" met the libertarian politics of Paris in May, 1968. Disputing Freud's pessimistic insistence on the triumph of the "death instinct," Marcuse believed the aim of this instinct was not aggression, but the end of the tension that was life. Its aim, said Marcuse, is not the termination of life, but of pain. Marcuse, a utopian, believed that the destructive aspects of the "death" and "life" instincts should be diverted from social control by the liberation of their energies. Aesthetic play should replace work. The sexual tyranny of the genitals used in reproduction would return to the state of the "polymorphous perversity" of the child. "Only with the entire body non-repressively re-eroticized, could alienated labor, grounded in the non-genital areas of the body, be overcome." Marcuse was a political anarchist, refusing all established order. His belief was that life could only be lived in the present.

The original scenario for Bow Wow Wow, which McLaren developed in Paris after the Sex Pistols, was a perverse, bisexual musical, performed by and, presumably for, pubescent children who acted out games on a "play" airplane trip. Titled "Mile High Club," it is a send-up of William Golding's *Lord of the Flies.* Nearly all the songs were written by McLaren, and many, such as "Sexy Eiffel Tower," dealt with child sexuality.

Sexuality in children, of course, is the last great taboo. While mother/child relations are acceptable images of pedophilia, any sexual relation between an older adult male and a female or male child is forbidden. Women's emotions (when not directed towards men) have been considered acceptable only when they are placed within the context of the patriarchal father/mother/child nuclear family unit. Otherwise, they are dangerous and threaten the sexual patriarchal family status quo. Women aren't allowed to love other women without being labeled deviant. Yet, on the other hand, daughters are expected to be subservient to the traditional values and love of their mothers.

McLaren's use of 14-year-old Annabella Lwin was wildly overdetermined, like an ad campaign for a new product. In films and advertising, "child nymphets" are used to eroticize childhood so that they can extend down to a (much) younger audience in the consumption of eroticized products. This has a dual appeal, both to adult, prurient interest in young girls (not unlike their appeal a century ago to Lewis Carroll), and to children themselves who are in touch with "sex" through the magic of the television image. Child nymphets, like Brooke Shields, were used to open up a new market of both child consumers and adults imitating or observing kids. Aimed ostensibly at newly "liberated" women and girls, the actual effect of such advertising was one of retrenchment and reversal of the values of the

ANNABELLA IN *CHICKEN* MAGAZINE, 1981.

early seventies Women's Movement, or more accurately, was a relegation to last year's fashion. McLaren's use of Annabella was a counter-spectacle in calculated symmetry to the appearance of Brooke Shields. Both young women were used to exploit the new buying power of the 13- to 17-year-old consumer.

Bow Wow Wow was packaged like any other new product. Their first song defined the "target market"—young teens and pre-teens on roller skates. "C30 C60 C90 GO!" gave them license to become producers by "pirating" the goods of the big corporation. Ironically, the LP was released by the biggest corporation in the entertainment field, EMI. The next irony was that EMI and McLaren translated the theme of home cassette recording into a prototypical solution of creative corporate packaging—an inexpensive 8-track, Bow Wow Wow cassette, sold at half the normal price and packaged, as described in the press release, in a "new, fashionable, cigarette-style, flip-top pack," designed to look like a bubble-gum or cigarette carton.

In the first single, the kids were cast as "pirates," stealing corporate images cheaply and using them for their own purposes. But clearly EMI, which released the song for its own profit, must also have fantasized itself as a pirate. The sense of a free marketeer as an anarchic pirate lingers in phrases such as "Captains of Industry." The imagery of piracy which Bow Wow Wow fashioned for themselves in their "C30 C60 C90 GO!" phase can be read as a fantasy by and about the record company for the media-consuming public.

Yet who really is exploited by McLaren, the kids, the corporation, or the media-consuming public? Are the teenage "pirates" really liberated by the possibilities of their new sexual and economic "freedom," or are they merely the tools of the record industry in an attempt to rebuild its market? Are the company and the public "conned" by McLaren, or do they, knowing it is a con, succumb to it passively as entertainment? Or being aesthetic formalists, do they separate McLaren's P.R. gamesmanship from the group's music? "Just because it's Situationism doesn't make it right," wrote Mary Harron in the *Manchester Guardian* of November, 1980, when the group first appeared. "This is the usual McLaren paradox because everything else—the music, the spirit—is very healthy.... The same was true of punk rock where eventually the kids took what they needed from McLaren's fantasies and used them for their own ends."

Although McLaren's exploitation of Annabella was set up like an advertisement for jeans, the producer's role was made obvious, revealing the exploitation of the public and the girl. The contradictions of McLaren's own desires, as well as those of the voyeuristic public, were exposed. The question became: is it McLaren, the public (for whom the spectacle was produced), the record industry or Annabella who first has access to the desire which is created in the production of Annabella's sexuality?

I don't mind singing lyrics as long as they aren't too harsh. It took me a while to get used to them. I thought they were offensive at first. I thought, what's all this stuff about sex? Sex, sex, sex! It's all in the brain, it's st-uuuupid! But they explained to me that it's less boring and something different from boring old love songs . . . I didn't want to be a singer. No I wanted to be an air stewardess and I still do. . . . I'm stuck [in this group] with this odd manager and I'm just a school girl. I don't want people to think I'm a sweetie 'cuz I'm not. I want to make my mark as a singing stewardess. I'd rather go around the world and meet people. Do it my way.

[My mother] was shocked at first when she heard "Sexy Eiffel Tower," she said, "Annabella, what are you doing?!" She was really shocked. . . . Then I explained to her that I meant it was falling. I know everyone thinks it was Malcolm's idea to get a sexual kind of turn on because I was breathing like having orgasms or something, but the actual thing is that I was supposed to be falling off the Eiffel Tower. That's what I'm actually singing about.

QUESTION: *But you're also singing, "I feel sexy . . ."*
ANNABELLA: *I know. That's the story. They're the lyrics. They're the words . . .*
QUESTION: *What does that mean to you?*
ANNABELLA: *The words express things, but they're just words to songs. I get a real happy feeling 'cuz I imagine how I'm falling . . . it's meant to be fun.*

The edge of perversity in Annabella's unawareness of the sexual voyeurism of her adult audience carries with it the image of McLaren, the puppeteer, pulling the strings. But, McLaren's role is a little different from that of a Hitchcock, a Louis Malle or a Godard. In fact, his scenarios work against certain media images, both by exploiting (using his performers as media bait), and deconstructing. Annabella and the other members of Bow Wow Wow are simultaneously exploited and left free to define and redefine the situation in their own terms and language. They resemble the teenage actors in Godard's films, such as *Le Gai Savoir* or *La Chinoise*, who were used to represent youth in general and Godard's script, but were also allowed to contradict these roles and to represent themselves.

BOY GEORGE AND ANNABELLA, 1980.

ANNABELLA: *I'm being exploited, but that's what you expect, isn't it?*
MATTHEW ASHMAN: *Nothing wrong with it . . . every 15-year-old is being exploited in some way. There are 15-year-olds in school being exploited, having school books shoved down their throats. . . . I think she's being exploited in a good way myself.*
ANNABELLA: *I don't know about a good way. But it's true what he says. "You're 15, and you're being exploited." Well, if I'm 16, will people still say I'm being exploited, or something? You know what I mean? I mean I don't think it really matters. I think it's stupid.*

Annabella's reaction to the controversy of the nearly-nude photo of her taken for the cover of the group's album—a recreation in the modern form of a fashion photograph of Edouard Manet's *Le dejeuner sur l'herbe* is a case in point.

The photograph shows two members of the group posed in white, romantic costumes, reclining next to Annabella, who is nude. A picnic lunch is spread out on the grass next to them. A third member of the group is wading in the pond and another is in a boat. The picturing of Annabella alludes to a broader iconography of French Romantic painting. The odalisque-like tilt of her head suggests work by Ingres, while the fact that Annabella's skin is "exotically" colored (hence "Oriental"), suggests a relation to another well-known painting by Manet entitled *Olympia*. In *Olympia*, the girlish prostitute is attended by a black serving maid. The prostitute and the black servant, both wearing highly fashionable, bourgeois clothes, were unsettling images to the nineteenth-century middle-class art public. In a Britain fearful of the loss of "Britishness" through interracial coupling, Annabella is unnervingly ambigious. Is she a normal, chaste British girl, or is she an "exotic" prostitute? In the iconography of the photograph, according to McLaren's critics, she is a child prostitute. Guitarist Matthew Ashman interprets Annabella as a prostitute only in the sense that every 15-year-old is similarly exploited by school and other social institutions. This reading was reinforced when McLaren released the photograph (after RCA had banned its use as an album cover) to a New York newspaper as a centerfold, entitling it "We're only in it for the Manet."

The furor developed by the photograph forced Annabella to make a choice between the conflicting loyalties she held to her mother, McLaren and the band. In the end, she chose the band over the two parental figures in conflict with each other. In an early interview, her main concern was her image in the press being in conflict with the "subjective" sincerity of her own intentions. She said, "that picture I thought was a good picture. It's not really pornographic. I *was* in the nude, but it's not as if I was showing anything. I think it's very artistic and very tasteful, beautiful to look at. A lot of people reckon it's a hell of a lot better than the painting."

When asked if she regretted doing it, she replied:

I did the picture because I was forced into it—I might as well be blunt with you—I was forced into it because at the time I wasn't really sure about doing it. But then I did the picture and there's no point in saying, "Oh, I'm really ashamed" because I'm not. In some ways I regret doing it because, even though I wasn't showing anything, I was in the nude. And to my mum, close people, friends of mine, they might think of me as cheap, "A cheap nymphet," I've been called in one paper. Which is a damn cheek, 'cuz I'm not, y'know? That's what makes me really sick about those cheap papers, 'cuz they just label me for some stupid reason. They've got no right to judge me. No one has . . . I'm the only girl in my family . . . I'm the youngest in my family . . . I would never do a picture like that again, because I don't want to hurt my family . . . My mum's very possessive over me, very protective.

Initially, Annabella was unaware of the nymphet role she was representing. In performance, during the simulated female orgasms of "Sexy Eiffel Tower" ("I'm coming! I'm coming!"), she would simply fall to the ground as if she were a doll. McLaren's theater was a place where choir boy actors were used in classically-delivered comedies to make sly references to contemporary scandals. The fact that such shameless truths were coming from innocent lips only gave the references added ironic meaning. McLaren used "bubble-gum" lyrics to openly express the pubescent, sexual fantasies of his hypothetical, eroticized schoolgirl audience. Are these "our" and McLaren's fantasies of a young girl's erotic dreams ("Louis Quatorze," "King Kong," "Sexy Eiffel Tower"), and not those of Annabella? How aware is she of her own sexuality and how aware is she of our gaze—a look which desires to know what she knows, her relative innocence or experience? Annabella explains:

I know what sex is about.... Everybody knows about it at my age. You talk about these things.... There's nothing disgusting about sex. [But] I hope it doesn't get any younger than 12, 'cause, I mean ... I'll be really shocked.... I think people should know about sex so they can handle it. Otherwise, they think it's silly and get all the wrong ideas.... It all depends on the individual. If girls want to sleep around, that's up to them.... I'm not a bloody nymphet.... What is a nymphet, anyway? If the press want a figure like that, they can find someone else. I don't happen to be that way. I don't see anything wrong in being like that, but I'm not. It worries me because you can't believe anything you read or what you're labeled as. That's why I'm doing this interview with you.... I don't think of things in terms of white and black. I despise that. It's like male chauvinists—men who really think women are weak and should get married, stay home.... It's like your being conditioned into it.... I don't mix with kids my age.... I don't go for the type of things that girls went for ... like all that talk about boys and going out with so and so ...

"Has she met anybody on the road?" "On the road!?" Annabella laughs incredulously at the thought, "You don't mix work, no, not on the road, not after a gig. It's like you wouldn't go out with people you interview. Obviously, if you were interviewing a woman who you thought was attractive, you couldn't say, 'Let's go out for a drink after we finish the interview.'" In her attitude is a necessary shield from the realization of how her sexuality is being exploited. Her naively chaste attitude, her lack of interest in other girls' interest in boys, are all actual expressions of her desire to gain self-identity on her own terms. The paradox is that this self-identity can only be gained through socially hierarchical identifications—being a mother's daughter or the female child sex object in a male-dominated rock band.

According to the *Guardian*, the spirit of Bow Wow Wow as simply kid's music was very healthy, whereas McLaren's political and commercial aspirations are suspect and distracting. The writer noted that "eventually [the kids] took what they needed from McLaren's fantasies and used them for their own ends." It is doubtful whether the kids were even concerned about McLaren's role. What is interesting is that the access on the part of a self-conscious, adult audience to a fantasy of pure, youth-oriented rock 'n' roll and to Annabella's pleasure is constantly blocked by McLaren's shadowy presence. McLaren's interests are continually getting in the way of our possession of the illusion. His "universal" presence is a constant reminder that both we and McLaren do not have anything more than a speculative/voyeuristic relation to child sexuality, that this sexuality, ultimately, can only be defined by Annabella and the male group members, as well as by the teenage audience.

McLaren's production of a spectacle gives the audience the illusion that we have given Annabella her sexuality. We are the parents of her desirability. McLaren's desire has produced this effect—of her erotic infinitude and the erotic infinitude of child sexuality— for us and for him. Annabella appears fascinating because our interest has been focused on her concealed, but visibly developing, sexuality. What we really desire to see is how female sexuality is produced. Our desire to identify female sexuality is a desire to represent Annabella's desire and our desire. It is also our desire to identify with the position from which her desire emanates.

Editor's note: This is a revised version of two essays previously published in *ZG* magazine (London) and *Real Life* magazine (New York).

CHRONOLOGY

Compiled by Malcolm McLaren

1946 Born London, January 22, to Emily Isaacs and Peter McLaren. Lives with grandmother Rose Corre.

1951 Enters school, but is removed by grandmother and instructed at home.

1955 Returns to school.

1966 Studies at Chiswick Polytechnic (affiliated with London Academy of Music and Dramatic Art); is expelled.

Meets Vivienne Westwood.

1967 Arrested with Henry Adler for attempting to burn an American flag in Grosvenor Square.

1968 Attends Croydon College of Art. Meets Robin Scott and Jamie Reid.

May: Students and workers riot in Paris; police intervention at the Sorbonne. McLaren frustrated in his attempts to go to Paris.

August: McLaren travels to Paris.

1973 Redesigns the shop, changing its name to *Too Fast To Live Too Young To Die*. Goes to New York with Westwood to attend a boutique fair at which they sell nothing. They meet the New York Dolls.

1974 Shop's name changed to *Sex*. Sells black rubber and leather fetish clothing. In the windows are exhibited paintings of life on the Left Bank in Paris during the 1950's, with references to the Lettrists and beatniks.

Begins managing a band called QT Jones and the Sex Pistols.

Goes to New York and manages the New York Dolls. Their singer, David Johansen, is given Mao's little red book, and asked to use the word red at least six times in every song. McLaren sees Richard Hell perform "Blank Generation" at CBGB.

1975 May: Returns to London; recasts the Sex Pistols with John Lydon as lead singer.

Summer: Exhibits clothing at the Institute of Contemporary Arts, London, featuring Karl Marx shirt.

November 6: Sex Pistols' first performance, at St. Martin's School of Art. Lasts 10 minutes.

Meets Jordan, who begins work at *Sex*. Designs bondage trousers with Westwood using U.S. army trousers and belt as the pattern.

Lives with Helen Wellington-Lloyd, who designs Sex Pistols leaflets, cutting up letters from newspapers to resemble ransom notes (a technique later refined by Jamie Reid).

1963 Attends evening classes at St. Martin's School of Art.

1964 Attends Harrow Art College. Spends most of his time in the British Museum. Impressed by exhibition featuring works of Andy Warhol. Leaves home and art school.

1965 Attends South East Essex and is expelled. Mounts an installation at Kingly Street Gallery, London: fills the space with a maze made of seven-foot high white corrugated cardboard which spills out onto the street, stops traffic, and finally closes the gallery.

1969 –71 Attends Goldsmiths' College. Meets Helen Wellington-Lloyd. Paints a series of pictures about punishments at school entitled "I Will Be So Bad."

Begins documentary on the history of Oxford Street. Script reads: From Tyburn at the gallows to the Gordon Riots and Barnaby Rudge to Nash and the rebuilding of the street, from its dangerous curves to a wide and perfectly straight highway, so an army could swiftly move down it without fear of ambush. For a new bourgeois to parade down it, to the invention of a cul-de-sac, and the doorman to trap and catch thieves on it. The coming of the department store and crowd control. The politics of boredom, and the fact that more Mars bars are sold on Oxford Street than anywhere else in the world. This is a journey in 24 hours of a life on Oxford Street.

Lacking funds, McLaren abandons the project. Begins designing clothes and collecting records, and leaves college without taking his finals.

1972 Opens boutique *Let it Rock* (named after a Chuck Berry song) at 430 King's Road. Persuades Vivienne Westwood to leave her teaching post and become a partner. They design costumes for Ken Russell's film *Mahler*, for the movie *That'll Be the Day* (starring David Essex and Ringo Starr), and for many television dance shows.

1976 *Sex* shop raided; charged along with Westwood for selling pornographic clothing.

Sex Pistols banned from the Marquee Club. McLaren hires Jamie Reid as graphic artist and finds venue for the Sex Pistols at El Paradise, a strip club in Soho, London.

November: Sex Pistols release the single "Anarchy in the U.K." on EMI records.

December 1: Group appears on Bill Grundy's "Today" Show; they use language considered unacceptable for TV broadcast, and are subsequently banned from live performance throughout the U.K.

1977 EMI fires the Sex Pistols. McLaren signs the group to Barclay label in Paris.

King's Road shop renamed *Seditionaries*; features studded bondage boots.

Sid Vicious replaces Glen Matlock on bass.

March 9: Sex Pistols sign with A & M.

March 16: Sex Pistols fired by A & M.

Sex Pistols sign with Virgin records. "God Save the Queen" single is released. The design for the cover of the single hits the front page on the eve of the Queen's Silver Jubilee. The Sex Pistols celebrate the occasion by following the Queen's flotilla with their own boat called the Queen Elizabeth, playing their version of "God Save the Queen." McLaren and Westwood arrested. "God Save the Queen" was number 1 on many charts despite the fact that it was banned by most radio stations.

July: Travels to Hollywood and meets film director Russ Meyer. Writes screenplay *Who Killed Bambi?* with Roger Ebert. Returns to London to raise money for the film. Meyer arrives in London, starts to shoot footage, but investors in the film cancel the project.

November 4: Virgin releases the LP *Never Mind the Bollocks*.

1978 January: The Sex Pistols undertake worldwide tour, but are still banned from the U.K. The tour is halted when they are banned from the U.S. Finally granted a 7-day visa through their U.S. label Warner Brothers. Tour the South—Atlanta, Memphis, San Antonio, Dallas, Tulsa—and finally San Francisco, where John Lydon leaves the band. Sex Pistols then banned from Finland, the second leg of the tour, which subsequently falls into chaos.

March: McLaren and Sex Pistols to Brazil; Steve Jones and Paul Cook meet exiled Australian train-robber Ronald Biggs; work begins on the film *The Great Rock 'n' Roll Swindle*. Biggs, replacing Johnny Rotten on lead vocals, records the single "No One is Innocent" with the group. Virgin Records refuses to release it, yet finally does under legal pressure; it reaches number 4 on the charts.

Johnny Rotten assumes his real name, John Lydon, and forms a new group, Public Image Limited. He brings suit against McLaren.

October 12: Sid Vicious is charged with killing his girlfriend Nancy Spungeon.

1979 February 2: Sid Vicious dies of a heroin overdose while out on bail.

February 10: First court appearance in case vs. Lydon, Virgin, and Warner Brothers. The funds of McLaren's companies, Glitterbest and Matrixbest, are put into official receivership.

McLaren unable to finish film *The Great Rock 'n' Roll Swindle*; removes his name from credits. Leaves for Paris, where he releases his first solo single on Barclay label, entitled "You Need Hands," from *The Great Rock 'n' Roll Swindle* soundtrack.

1982 McLaren stops managing Bow Wow Wow. McLaren and Westwood exhibit a new fashion collection, "Buffalo Gals," both in London and Paris, featuring an ethnic dance and hobo look.

New shop opened at St. Christopher's Place. McLaren designs its facade, a brown clay relief of the world, and calls the shop *Nostalgia of Mud*.

Releases single "Buffalo Gals."

Together with Westwood, shows a new fashion collection called "Punkature" in London and Paris.

1983 Releases album *Duck Rock*.

Last collection together with Westwood, featured in Paris only, with prints by Keith Haring and music mixing rap and opera.

1984 Charisma releases McLaren's second LP, *Fans*, which combines arias from *Madame Butterfly* and *Carmen* set in a Rhythm & Blues format.

Westwood and McLaren split.

1985 Leaves for New York; finally settles in Hollywood. Works for CBS films developing movies such as *All She Wants To Do Is Surf With Nazis* and *Fashionbeast*. Devises the stage show *Fans* based on the album.

1980 Returns to London.

The Great Rock 'n' Roll Swindle film released, credited only to Julien Temple.

Using images of Blackbeard and Geronimo with the sound of black urban rap and dance, McLaren produces Adam Ant and Bow Wow Wow.

King's Road shop renamed *World's End*.

Writes a song for Bow Wow Wow, "C30 C60 C90 GO!" which advocates home-taping from the radio. Produces video for EMI with Bow Wow Wow dressed as pirates. Single hits the top 20, but EMI stops pressing it. Adam Ant releases *King of the Wild Frontier*. Lieutenant Lush, also known as Boy George, appears with Bow Wow Wow at a fun fair concert at the Rainbow Theater. McLaren and Boy George write a song entitled "The Mile High Club." EMI releases Bow Wow Wow's *Your Cassette Pet—Flip Pack Pop*.

November: McLaren and Westwood stage their first fashion collection, "Pirates." RCA signs Bow Wow Wow. McLaren writes lyrics for song called "Go Wild in the Country," based on "Craft must have clothes but truth loves to go naked." Annabella, the 14-year-old lead singer of Bow Wow Wow, appears nude in a photo recreation of Manet's *Dejeuner sur l'herbe* on album cover. RCA does not release the cover. McLaren and Westwood stage new collection called "Savage," including prints with Apache Indian designs.

1981 Records a country and western singer, She Sherriff. Charisma releases the single "I Forgot More Than You'll Ever Know About Him," then fires She Sherriff and signs McLaren instead. McLaren hires Trevor Horn and goes around the world to record his first solo album.

1986 On trial in London to resolve questions of rights to the Sex Pistols' profits. Refusing to fight an extended court battle, walks out of court and gives up rights to the Sex Pistols name.

1987 Signs with CBS records in London to make an album with Jeff Beck based on waltzes, co-produced by Bootsy Collins to be released in 1988.

1988 In Hollywood, develops the musical *Fans*, produced by Stevie Phillips, directed by Tommy Tune, written by McLaren and Menno Meyjes, with lyrics by McLaren adapted from his album. Scheduled for Broadway premiere in 1989.

Co-produces *New Rose Hotel* with Ed Pressman, a film directed by Katherine Bigelow; screenplay by William Gibson, based on a short story of the same name.

Developing musical film with Amblin productions based on his own music.

LIST OF ILLUSTRATIONS

Front Cover
Malcolm McLaren being arrested during the Queen's Jubilee Celebration, 1977. Photo: Luciana Martinez de la Rosa

Inside Front Cover
McLaren in *Let It Rock*, 1972. Photo: David Parkinson

The New York Dolls' Red Show, 1975. Photo: Bob Gruen/Star File

Sex Pistols, *Never Mind the Bollocks, Here's the Sex Pistols*, album cover, design by Jamie Reid, 1977. Courtesy Virgin Records Ltd.

Poster for Sex Pistols single, "Pretty Vacant," design by Jamie Reid, 1977. Courtesy Virgin Records Ltd.

Sid Vicious and Johnny Rotten during Sex Pistols U.S. tour, 1978. Photo: Annie Leibovitz

T-shirt with chicken bones, design by Vivienne Westwood and McLaren, 1973.

Page 15
McLaren in Tennessee, 1983. Photo: Bob Gruen/Star File

Page 19
Malcolm McLaren, installation in parking lot, 1967.

McLaren at Croydon College of Art, 1967.

Page 21
Film still from Andy Warhol's *Vinyl*, 1965. Photo: courtesy of the Whitney Museum of American Art

Cover, *King Mob Echo*, No. 1, April 1968.

Page 22
Still from Bob Grundy's "Today" Show, London; Johnny Rotten (left), Steve Jones (right), 1976.

Sex Pistols, "Anarchy in the U.K.," single cover, design by Jamie Reid, 1977. Courtesy Virgin Records Ltd.

Page 23
Animation still from *The Great Rock 'n' Roll Swindle*, 1979–80. Courtesy Virgin Vision

Page 24
Sex Pistols, "God Save the Queen," single cover, design by Jamie Reid, 1977. Courtesy Virgin Records Ltd.

Cover, *Investors Review*, Sex Pistols named "Young Businessmen of the Year," 1977.

Page 25
Film still from *The Great Rock 'n' Roll Swindle*, 1979–80. Courtesy Virgin Vision

Page 26
Adam and the Ants, *King of the Wild Frontier*, album cover, front and back, 1980.

Page 27
Johnny Rotten, 1978. Photo: Annie Leibovitz

Page 28
Sid Vicious in a film still from *The Great Rock 'n' Roll Swindle*, 1979–80. Courtesy Virgin Vision

Video still from *Madam Butterfly*, directed by Terry Donovan, 1984.

Page 34
Vivienne Westwood and McLaren in *Let It Rock*, 1972. Photo: David Parkinson

Page 36
McLaren in Teddy-Boy suit, 1972.

Page 37
Sex shop exterior, 1975. Photo: Bob Gruen/Star File

Page 38
Seditionaries interior, 1977.

Page 40
Sketch for *World's End* shop front, David Connor, 1980.

World's End shop front, 1980.

Steve Strange modelling pirate outfit, design by Vivienne Westwood and McLaren, 1981. Photo: Robyn Beeche

Page 42
Nostalgia of Mud shop front, London, 1982.

Page 43
Nostalgia of Mud shop front London, 1982. (Detail)

Page 48
New York Dolls, *Red Patent Leather*, album cover, 1974. Photo: Bob Gruen

McLaren in company of Bernie Rhodes, and Martie Thau, manager of the New York Dolls. Photo: Bob Gruen/Star File

Page 50
McLaren and the original Sex Pistols at EMI contract signing, 1976. Photo: Bob Gruen/Star File

Page 51
McLaren and the Sex Pistols at the A & M press conference, March 1977. Photo: Ray Stevenson

Sex Pistols "Pretty Vacant," single cover, design by Jamie Reid, 1977. Courtesy Virgin Records Ltd.

Page 53
Three T-shirts, design by Vivienne Westwood and McLaren, 1973–76.

Page 55
Still from Russ Meyer's footage for the proposed Sex Pistols film, as reproduced on *The Great Rock 'n' Roll Swindle* soundtrack album, back cover, 1980. Courtesy Virgin Records Ltd.

Page 56
Andy Warhol, *Sid Vicious* cover, *Art & Text* and *File* magazines joint issue, 1986.

Page 60
Bow Wow Wow promotional photograph, 1981. Photo: Andy Earl

Page 63
Bow Wow Wow promotional booklet, 1981. Design: Nick Egan

Page 65
Promotional photograph of Annabella from *Chicken* magazine, 1981.

Page 68
Boy George and Annabella, 1980. Photo: Kevin Cummins

Page 80
McLaren, Vivienne Westwood and model in *World's End* garments featuring Keith Haring design. Photo: Steven Meisel; Courtesy *Vogue*. ©1983 Condé Nast Publications Inc.

Inside Back Cover
Malcolm McLaren, 1988. Photo: Michael Halsband

"Buffalo Gal" outfit, design by Vivienne Westwood and McLaren, 1983.

Malcolm McLaren, *Duck Rock*, album cover, 1983.

Bow Wow Wow album cover, *See Jungle! See Jungle! Go Join Our Gang Yeah, City All Over! Go Ape Crazy!*, 1981. Photo: Andy Earl

Malcolm McLaren, *Fans*, album cover, design by Nick Egan, 1984.

Bow Wow Wow, *See Jungle! See Jungle! Go Join Our Gang Yeah, City All Over! Go Ape Crazy!*, album cover graphic, 1981.

Back Cover
Malcolm McLaren, 1985. Photo: Annie Leibovitz

BOARD OF TRUSTEES

Jay Chiat

Gregory C. Clark

Maureen Cogan

Elaine Dannheisser

Richard Ekstract

Arthur A. Goldberg
Treasurer

Allen Goldring

Paul C. Harper, Jr.

Sharon King Hoge

Martin Kantor

Nanette Laitman

Vera G. List
Vice President

Henry Luce, III
President

Raymond J. McGuire

Patrick Savin

Paul Schnell

Herman Schwartzman, Esq.

Laura Skoler

Marcia Tucker

STAFF

Kimball Augustus
Security

Richard Barr
Volunteer Coordinator

Virginia Bowen
Public Affairs Intern

Jeanne Breitbart
Assistant, Curatorial Department

Teresa Bramlette
Curatorial Secretary

Gayle Brandel
Administrator

Susan Cahan
Education Coordinator

Helen Carr
Special Events Coordinator

Russell Ferguson
Librarian

Angelika Festa
Assistant to the Librarian

Karen Fiss
Curatorial Coordinator

Thomas Freeman
Operations Manager

Maren Hensler
Art Quest/New Collectors Coordinator

Ellen Holtzman
Managing Director

Popsy Johnston
Art Quest/New Collectors Coordinator

Elon Joseph
Security

Gayle Kurtz
Docent Coordinator

Margo Machida
Assistant to the Director of Planning and Development

Clare Micuda
Assistant to the Director

Judith Morris
Receptionist

Jill L. Newmark
Registrar

Barbara Niblock
Bookkeeper

William Olander
Senior Curator

Sara Palmer
Director of Public Affairs

Wayne Rottman
Registrarial/Operations Assistant

Aleya Saad
Planning and Development Assistant

Cindy Smith
Preparator/Assistant to the Registrar

Susan Stein
Admissions Coordinator

Virginia Strull
Director of Planning and Development

Neville Thompson
Assistant to the Operations Manager

Laura Trippi
Assistant Curator

Marcia Tucker
Director

Suzanna Watkins
Assistant to the Administrator

Margaret Weissbach
Coordinator of Docents and Interns

Alice Yang
Curatorial Coordinator

MCLAREN, WESTWOOD AND MODEL IN *WORLD'S END* GARMENTS, FEATURING KEITH HARING DESIGN, 1983.

Catalog © 1988 The New Museum of Contemporary Art, New York
All rights reserved. No part of this book may be reproduced in any form by
electronic or mechanical means (including photocopying, recording or information
storage and retrieval) without permission in writing from the publisher.

Library of Congress Catalog Number: 88-043017; ISBN: 0-262-70035-2

LIBRARY OF DAVIDSON COLLEGE

Books on regular loan may be checked out for **two weeks.** Books must be presented at the Circulation Desk in order to be renewed.

A fine is charged after date due.

Special books are subject to special regulations at the discretion of the library staff.